Mindfulness Training

How Changing Lifestyle Can Improve Our Health

(The Ultimate Guides on Mindfulness Meditation Techniques)

Shaun Peters

Published by Rob Miles

© **Shaun Peters**

All Rights Reserved

Mindfulness Training: How Changing Lifestyle Can Improve Our Health (The Ultimate Guides on Mindfulness Meditation Techniques)

ISBN 978-1-990084-08-9

All rights reserved. No part of this guide may be reproduced in any form without permission in writing from the publisher except in the case of brief quotations embodied in critical articles or reviews.

Legal & Disclaimer

The information contained in this book is not designed to replace or take the place of any form of medicine or professional medical advice. The information in this book has been provided for educational and entertainment purposes only.

The information contained in this book has been compiled from sources deemed reliable, and it is accurate to the best of the Author's knowledge; however, the Author cannot guarantee its accuracy and validity and cannot be held liable for any errors or omissions. Changes are periodically made to this book. You must consult your doctor or get professional medical advice before using any of the suggested remedies, techniques, or information in this book.

Upon using the information contained in this book, you agree to hold harmless the Author from and against any damages, costs, and expenses, including any legal fees potentially resulting from the application of any of the information provided by this guide. This disclaimer applies to any damages or injury caused by the use and application, whether directly or indirectly, of any advice or information presented, whether for breach of contract, tort, negligence, personal injury, criminal intent, or under any other cause of action.

You agree to accept all risks of using the information presented inside this book. You need to consult a professional medical practitioner in order to ensure you are both able and healthy enough to participate in this program.

Table of Contents

INTRODUCTION 1

CHAPTER 1: SEIZE TIME AWAY 2

CHAPTER 2: WHAT IS MINDFULNESS MEDITATION? 6

CHAPTER 3: PILLARS OF MEDITATION 27

CHAPTER 4: BOOST YOUR CAREER WITH MINDFULNESS . 35

CHAPTER 5: ALWAYS REMEMBER THESE TIPS & TRICKS .. 39

CHAPTER 6: THE EMOTIONAL BENEFITS OF MEDITATION 46

CHAPTER 7: TEN OF THE MOST EFFECTIVE MINDFULNESS EXERCISES TO BE IN A CONSTANT STATE OF HAPPINESS . 56

CHAPTER 8: MINDFULNESS AND PRACTICALITY 65

CHAPTER 9: THE POWER OF YOUR MIND 85

CHAPTER 10: MINDFULLNESS TO MINDFREENESS - LEADING TO A LIFE OF JOY 97

CHAPTER 11: MINDFULNESS OF THE ENVIRONMENT AND CIRCUMSTANCES 104

CHAPTER 12: EQUANIMITY 109

CHAPTER 13: HOW TO THINK ABOUT FAILURE AND RISK THE HEALTHY WAY 117

CHAPTER 14: LEAVE THEM BEHIND 121

CHAPTER 15: 7 MINDFULNESS TECHNIQUES TO REMAIN MINDFUL AT ANY GIVEN MOMENT 126

CHAPTER 16: ELIMINATING STRESS 145

CHAPTER 17: ELIMINATING STRESS 152

CHAPTER 18: POWERFUL HABIT CHANGES FOR A BETTER LIFE 158

CHAPTER 19: MINDFULNESS MEDITATION TO HELP COPE WITH PHYSICAL PAIN 176

CHAPTER 20: CONTINUING YOUR MINDFUL GROWTH JOURNEY 184

CONCLUSION 188

Introduction

This book is the definitive guide to get you on your way to becoming at one with the universe in a way that bestows peace while you understand the concept of mindfulness and meditation. The steps in this book will get you to understand how to go about understanding your inner self and create a path to mindfulness and mindful meditation.

Thanks again for downloading this book, I hope you enjoy it!

Chapter 1: Seize Time Away

When Thoreau went to the woods surrounding Walden Pond, it was to listen to the frogs. His work with the Emerson family in Concord meant he lived with them. He craved solitude. The Emersons had four children. Children tend to disrupt quiet with enthusiasm.

His fidgety mind compelled him to live alone and, at first, he wasn't sure what he needed to discover. That's the way most of us begin our journey with mindful practice. We ache for something different; we're just not clear what it looks like.

In the woods, Thoreau learned the incomparable value of being. In his first year, he didn't read or write much. He grew beans. He fished. He walked. He sat, and looked and listened. He turned the piercing whistle of the steam locomotive into an experience as natural as the sun rising and the hawk screeching. He literally built new proteins in his brain.

The first way to be mindful is to seize time away from the routines of ordinary life, especially in the midst of everyday living. Thoreau's circumstances in Concord seem idyllic in comparison to our commutes, job stress, family drama and the pace of modern life. His example, therefore, applies even more to us.

You can only get a break from whatever is stressful to you if you take the time. Your brain reacts during periods of stress. It doesn't think or savor. It can't turn down because it doesn't know it's allowed to. It's when we step back from our lives long enough to differentiate between the stressful and the sublime that we begin the path to every moment being mindful.

Thoreau's mindfulness started with time away to do nothing. The fact that the next year was his most prolific and arguably his most powerful as a writer is not an accident. Mindfulness became natural.

What he had to do as an intentional exercise became a way of life and ultimately allowed him to be the creative person he wanted to be.

And the total experience of those two years, two months, and two days guided the rest of his career. He wrote prolifically. He fought slavery. He created the language, philosophy, and discipline of what today we call environmentalism. Through his family's business, he made great pencils. He chose his path and savored what he found along the way.

Can you imagine two years and two months, mostly alone, living simply? Most of us can't imagine two minutes without checking our smart phones, but we have to. Our world has evolved; our brains haven't caught up.

Eventually, with enough practice, the alarm only goes off when it needs to. When something demands your attention. When there is a real emergency. When our life is out of balance. If we're not afraid of stress because we realize it is our alarm trying to help us, even stress becomes an experience we value.

To begin building a relationship with your alarm, you can take a longer retreat like Henry did — a day, a week, even a year long sabbatical. You can snooze your technology each night at 7pm to get the downtime you need. You can make time between meetings to sit outside and quietly observe the world.

However you seize time away, once you recognize the contrast between real bears and those that are figments of a busy life, your alarm becomes an asset. It will let the parts of your brain that create calm and well-being run the show more often. You will begin, slowly, and eventually almost all the time, to feel better wherever you are, whatever you do.

Chapter 2: What Is Mindfulness Meditation?

It does not really matter whether you are thinking about school, work, or family life; it is so easy to be caught in a certain pattern of swirling thoughts. At times, we ruminate on the past events, even to the extent of plunging ourselves in anxiety, or we even opt to focus on the could-be situations that are impending. Mindfulness meditation can be defined as the mental training practice that can very helpful in situations such as these. It will bring you and your thoughts into the present, making you focus on the sensations, thoughts, and emotions that you are undergoing at the moment.

Whereas it can be not so easy to silent the thoughts, with practice and patience, you will be able to experience the benefits of mindfulness meditation that include less anxiety, stress, as well as alleviated conditions such as the IBS. The methodologies can range, but in general, mindfulness meditation includes mental imagery, breathing practice, body and muscle relaxation, and awareness of mind and body.

Mindfulness meditation has been around for a very long time. But despite that extended period that it has been around, its origin is still not known. Instructions for mindfulness meditation have been discovered in the ancient texts of almost every major religion including Christianity, Judaism, and even Buddhism. It is, however, Buddhism that can really assist us to comprehend the origin of mindfulness meditation. This is due to the fact that the practice itself is integral to the main path of Buddhist. It is very important in Buddhism to cultivate a non-judgmental awareness of your surroundings, your mind, your feelings, and most importantly, yourself. This observation and distance can still be trained through a number of mindfulness meditations.

For a number of religions, mindfulness meditation was applied as a means of stepping back from the environment and connecting with the spiritual self. At times, this kind of connection was used as a means of resisting temptation, whereas other times it was used as a way of realizing and understanding the connection between other and self. As of today, the meaning of mindfulness meditation has moved away from its religious inclinations. Whereas there are some people who still practice it within the context of religion, mindfulness meditation has been adopted by healthcare professionals, psychologists, as well as other secular organizations as one of the most effective means of dealing with the illnesses and stresses of the modern day world.

Despite the fact that many special styles and methodologies have been created, all mindfulness meditations possess the following common features:

Non-judgmental is essential – All mindfulness meditations tend to focus on experiencing awareness without passing certain forms of judgment. Mindfulness, in other words, is all about witnessing a sensation or experience without any form of critic and attachment.

Awareness is Key – The main focus of all mindfulness meditation is the process of developing awareness. At times, this awareness is of the breath and body, whereas other times it could tend to focus on the internal thoughts and the outside world.

Mindfulness Cultivates Peace – Witnessing a particular thing without attaching value or meaning creates a very vital detachment that would results in a peaceful and calm mind. Even though your feelings are important and valuable, mindfulness will still teach you how to attain serenity despite all that.

One of the original standardized programs for mindfulness meditation has been the MBSR - Mindfulness-Based Stress Reduction. The program was created by Dr. Jon Kabat-Zinn, who was a student of Thich Nhat, a Buddhist scholar, and monk. The 8-week long program that he designed was meant to guide the students on how to pay attention to the current, lower arousal and reactivity, and attain a state of calm. There is also a number of other more secular, simplified meditation interventions that have been increasingly included in the medical setting for the purposes of treating pain, stress, and depression among a number of other conditions.

Despite the fact that the spiritual effects of mindfulness meditation are well recognized, there are still scientifically proven and profound physical and emotional benefits. A number of these benefits have just recently started to be studied, however, the past decade has witnessed a great shift when it comes to understanding how mindfulness meditation operates, how it influences the brain and the subsequent benefits and results are. Before you actually get started with your practice of mindfulness meditation, you may need to know some of the benefits that you can expect.

It is important to note that mindfulness is an extremely effective tool when it comes to dealing with the stress-based reactions such as generalized worry, insomnia, obsessive thinking, depression, and anxiety. There is one team of researches that analyzed data obtained from close to forty studies on the topic of mindfulness meditation. They discovered that 95% of the study participants got relief from the stress-based symptoms that they had after experimenting with mindfulness meditation. The most incredible result from that particular study is in regards to those who were affected.

As it came out openly, a number of weeks spent in treatment, age, as well as the kind of methodology did not have any effect on the results, and some of the vast majority of those who took part in the study retained their positive results once the study came to an end. It has been widely known that mindfulness will make you feel great, but now the scientists and researchers have managed to prove that mindfulness practice is one of the best things you can perform to be able to heal your emotional life.

The Difference Between Mindfulness and Meditation

Before anything else, it is important to note that both mindfulness and meditation are rooted in the traditional Buddhism. However, meditation is the larger term that is used to encompass mindfulness amid a number of other methodologies.

The terms mindfulness and meditation are tossed around quite much these days.

Oftentimes, the terms are interchangeably used, and at times, in their simplified forms, make references to just one general thing, which is the idea of calming a mind that has been frenzied. The differences that exist between these two terms have been interpreted and debated in a number of ways, and it appears that the debate is not coming down any time soon. They are just two sides of the same coin, and they also complement each other and even overlap at certain times. At the same time, each of these has its own purpose and definition.

For some time now, the whole zen thing has really been moving up. It appears like everybody is now rolling out their yoga mats, and updating their Instagram pages with captions such as "be mindful, and be in the present". However, it is important to note that just because the wellness has officially reached the masses, things do not get less confusing. It is still complicated, especially when it comes to the subtle distinction between mindfulness and meditation. To get things clear, there is a reason why people tend to confuse these two terms. It is due to the fact that both of them have various definitions, and they are also intertwined in a number of ways.

Despite the fact that it is often a fine line, there is still some difference between these two terms – meditation and mindfulness. Meditation can be described as a large umbrella word that includes the practice of hitting ultimate concentration and consciousness, to self-regulate the mind and acknowledge it. It can also include a number of methodologies to attain this heightened degree of consciousness, including mindfulness, patience, love, and of course, compassion. Therefore, mindfulness is a kind of meditation alongside other practices such as emptiness, breathing, silence, sexuality, yoga, and tantra. Mindfulness is basically the act of focusing on staying in the present, like taking time to focus entirely on drinking a hot cup of coffee, removing and tasting empowering emotions from the mind.

Meditation as a practice predates the idea of mindfulness, while mindfulness is usually aligned with the time of the Buddha, where the Buddha discovered that focusing wholly on the breath would enable one to discover the reality and attain meditation much faster.

In any specific day, there are certain times where nothing is really going on. However, we try to link up the events of the time from one thought to another without even giving a space. We even tend to overlook the kind of spaciousness that is all occurring in this excerpt is from a book that is known as the Unexpected Power of Mindfulness and Mindfulness.

The fact that meditation and mindfulness are today used to give the same meaning has really mixed up things. Mindfulness is the act of being aware. It is not only paying attention to the behavior, feelings, and thoughts, but also noticing the mentioned traits. Mindfulness can be practiced at any given time, at any place we are, without considering the people we are with, and whatever we are doing, so that we can be entirely present without any kind of distraction. This means that we become free of not only the present but also the future, free from what maybe's and what if's, as well as being free of judgment of wrong and right.

According to Jon Kabat-Zinn, mindfulness is basically the awareness that comes up each time we pay attention in the current moment in a non-judgmental manner. It basically cultivates access to the main aspects of our own bodies and minds that our sanity relies on. Mindfulness tends to restore the dimensions of our being due to the fact that it includes kindness and tenderness towards ourselves. The mentioned have never been missing, but we have just been absorbed somewhere else. Zinn, who authored the Unexpected Power of Mindfulness Meditation, went ahead to add some very important point. He says that each time a mind clarifies and opens, the heart will also clarify and opens.

Mindfulness also releases the happy chemicals in the brain, and also relaxes the tension that is around pain, improves digestion and reduces blood pressure. Mindfulness is so easy to practice and its effects are very amazing. It is not really bad when all that is required of us is to just pay attention, which is what we should all be doing but tend to forget. Each time, we pay attention; change becomes so easy to effect.

Meditation and mindfulness can just be referred to as the mirror-like reflections of each other. Meditation expands and nurtures mindfulness while mindfulness enriches and supports meditation. While meditation is always practiced for a given amount of time, mindfulness can be used in any situation all across the day. Mindfulness can be described as the awareness of certain things, whereas meditation is the awareness of nothing.

There are several forms of meditation. Some of the forms are aimed at creating a focused and clear mind, referred to as Clear Mind meditation. Others are also aimed at developing some altruistic states that include forgiveness, compassion, and loving-kindness. They are also referred to as the open-heart kind of meditation. Other forms of meditation also use the body as a way of developing awareness, such as walking and yoga; others also use sound, as in intoning sacred words and chanting.

Mindfulness meditation is therefore a type of clear mind meditation. Attention is usually paid to the natural rhythm of the breath while sitting, as well as to the rhythm of walking slowly. This, on its own, can have a very huge impact on your life.

At the end, the method is just an aide; and it is not really the experience. The fact that a hammer can help build a house does not really mean that it is the house. In the same manner, the practice of meditation is not an end on its own. At times, we may wander off and even do all manners of other things, but there will always be some sort of stillness.

It is not easy to grab a lifestyle magazine without coming across the mention of the main benefits of meditation and mindfulness. You will experience the same each time you go through your yoga-related social media pages. It would be very important to debunk the following common myths: mindfulness is not thinking so hard about something. On the other hand, meditation is not all about shutting down the mind like an off switch, which might appear so boring. The two practices are life skills whose main aim is to offer you the tools needed for accessing inner peace. They also depend on the ability to be entirely focused on the current moment. They also offer a way of lowering suffering and increasing happiness.

We are living in a point of time where eastern philosophy is starting to get into the mainstream western way of life. Words such as meditation and mindfulness are already forming part of the day-to-day conversations. But the question that rises up is if these words are really interchangeable. Since these terms are often used in a similar context, confusion concerning their differences is entirely understandable.

Health Benefits of Combining the Two

According to a meditation author and a teacher, Lodro Rinzler, mindfulness is just another type of meditation. As highlighted throughout the eBook, there are various forms of meditation, and they include visualization and contemplation, but mindfulness is the kind where you introduce your whole mind to a given object. You can improve your awareness of being in the present by following your breath. This is what is known as mindfulness meditation. Among the Buddhists, it is known as Shamatha. Rinzler also adds that eating could also be an additional way of practicing mindfulness. He says that a person can be mindful of their food, while tasting it, and when they finally drift off into all kinds of thoughts, they return to taste the food again. That is what can be referred to as the act of mindfulness.

Rinzler also explains that the whole process of meditation can predate the idea of mindfulness. In most cases, it is aligned with the "Buddha's time", where the Buddha himself discovered that wholly focusing on his breath would enable him to see the reality and attain meditation more efficiently.

Fast track to the modern age, the world witnessed the 5 mindfulness trainings, courtesy of a Vietnamese Buddhist monk,

Thich Nhat Hanh. He is also well known for his teachings on mindfulness.

It does not really matter whether you desire to learn about the various methodologies of meditation, or maybe you just want to be more mindful in your day to day life to lower stress, there is still a number of evidence that you can use to help in harnessing your mind to be in the present, and also improve both your physical and mental health.

A recent study on this topic discovered that those who practice mindfulness had healthier levels of glucose; implying self-focus and improved focus could help in fighting unhealthy eating habits and obesity. In addition to that, it has also been discovered that mindfulness meditation has some relationships to improved qualities of life among older adults who, in other instances, would be using pills. It has also been linked to lowered dependency on opioid drugs, improved focus, as well as reduced levels of depression and anxiety. But perhaps one thing that is very remarkable is the fact that positive thinking and mindfulness have a beneficial effect of mindfulness meditation on the body.

So, Where Does the Confusion Occurs?

The mix-up lies in the fact that one of the most universally recognized types of meditation is known as mindfulness meditation. As noted at the beginning of this eBook, mindfulness is just being in the know, and a person can choose to practice it formally or informally. And this is what most people do not understand. When you opt to practice it in an informal way, it implies that you are just trying to be more aware of all the things that you do. That mentality can, at times, be infused into nearly everything.

However, mindfulness practice is what is known as mindfulness meditation. But wait. What is mindfulness meditation in this context? It is when you intend to pay attention to anything that is here at the moment. The main goal is to learn how to be present, to an extent of feeling yourself reacting a kind of way at the moment later on. You become so much aware of the present moment that you are then able to take some step back, and even alter your knee-jerk reaction to be able to do something that is entirely different.

Now that the point is home, here is a quick summary of the two intertwined terms. Meditation is when a person intentionally schedules a time to perform certain errands that are beneficial to them, and there are nearly all types of meditation. On the other hand, mindfulness is both a formal practice of meditation and general awareness of the entire earth. As long as you are doing something that you believe is good for you, and on purpose, then that is what can be defined as meditation. For example, there is exercise meditation, where a person intentionally set out to exercise to have the mind unclogged. There is also what is referred to as a prayer meditation, where a person intentionally sends prayers out to the universe. Do not forget that there is also the music meditation where the entire goal is to offer ultimate relaxation.

It is actually two things, and not one, which is one of the most popular kinds of meditation.

Merging Mindfulness and Meditation

From the above information, it is clear that practicing mindfulness can easily lead to developing a meditation spirit. A meditation session is basically a highly focused amount of time where a person gets entirely mindful of themselves as living beings, and yet get themselves lost in just existing. The two merge together quite well, and they can substantially enrich your general life and your understanding of yourself as well as that of other people.

So, you should try to incorporate just a bit of mindfulness into just one of your day-to-day behaviors. It could be the time you spend as you prepare for work, or your breathing pattern when you practice yoga. You should take each step and carry it out not only with joy, but also with great purpose. Check if this will change your perception of the world that is around you or even your mood, and see if it can still be possible to bring it to more of the daily behaviors that you take part in. after that, you can take the next step and see if it is possible to carve out a little amount of time for meditation, maybe immediately after waking up or before retiring to bed.

Chapter 3: Pillars Of Meditation

There are many proven benefits of meditation. It's now a well-known fact that through meditation we can alleviate stress, enhance positive moods, sleep better, and more effectively deal with anxiety. Following the fame surrounding meditation, this is something that you may have tried. Perhaps, you tried this practice with the hope of gaining these and many more of the benefits associated with it, but then you lost hope. Chances are that you are thinking meditation is not your thing or that you are not good at it. This happens to most people because they fail to understand the vital pillars of meditation.

Three Fundamentals of Meditation

Your practice of meditation can only be successful if you fully understand the three essentials of meditation. They include:

- Habit

- Technique
- Application

Simply put, it is crucial that you practice meditation regularly by utilizing the right technique and ensuring that you apply the skills obtained in real life. Sounds simple, right? Well, let's dig in deeper to understand what meditation pillars are and why they are relevant as you begin practicing meditation.

Habit

For meditation to work for you, it is imperative that you practice it daily. Consider it to be food for your mind. You have to remember to feed it daily for optimal results. It is a habit that you need to develop from the get-go. Why is this essential? The main reason why you need to meditate daily is that you go through life's situations on a daily basis. Therefore, you need to constantly meditate to confirm that you are in a better position to deal with the negative thoughts that are part of life. Bear in mind that your ego is also always in action. So, meditating daily is a prerequisite. Without this, it will be challenging for you to keep up. You will find it challenging to connect with your inner self. Hence, it is better if you break down the process to a daily routine. After all, at no time will anxiety go on a holiday.

You might be asking yourself why you can't meditate just once or twice a week. Sure, you will experience the advantages of meditation if you adopt this routine. Nonetheless, it should be made clear that you will not unlock the full potential of daily meditation. What's more, the positive changes you will experience in your life will not last since you are not in full momentum.

Take a practical example where you want to boil water. In this case, the best way of boiling your water will be to leave it for about 6 minutes. This gives it enough time to reach its boiling point. Now, assume you heat the water for 3 minutes, then allow it to cool, and later heat it again for another 3 minutes. Clearly, the water will never reach its boiling point. You can continue doing this for weeks, but the outcome will be the same. Do you get the point here? For meditation to help you transform, you should practice it daily. Practice makes perfect.

Meditating daily doesn't have to sound like a hard task for you. Sparing a few minutes in your busy schedule will make a huge difference. It doesn't need to be several hours long; it can be as short as 5 minutes. The key issue is that you should do it daily.

Technique

You might meditate daily, but if you are using the wrong technique, then all your efforts will be in vain. Using the right meditation technique to suit you is vital. This doesn't mean that there are certain methods which are better than others. There are various forms of meditation, all with distinct benefits. When looking for the best approach, you need to keep in mind that your taste matters a lot.

The best way of determining whether a particular method is good for you or not is by experimenting. Try out several meditation techniques before you settle on the one you think serves you the best. Depending on the approach you use, you will realize that these techniques differ in how they make you feel, act, and behave. For instance, some of them will make you feel grounded whereas others will lift your energy. Others will evoke a passive mood while others will energize you. Concerning your professional life, some meditations will help you boost your productivity. On the other hand, some will take on a more spiritual outlook. Therefore, you need to experiment first before making up your mind.

You also need to understand that the right approach matters a great deal. In this case, it is crucial that you have the right attitude toward your practice. So, what should you be concerned about here?

Purpose

Besides making sure that you are using the right meditation technique, it is essential that you have the right purpose in mind. This means your practice should be fueled by interest, and no one should force or push you around to do it. It ought to come from within.

Pleasantness

Moreover, make your meditation an exciting experience. Doing this guarantees that you won't blame yourself if you happen to get distracted.

Perseverance

As mentioned earlier, meditating daily is an essential part of learning to successfully meditate. It will not be easy from the start, but you have to keep going. There are times when you will feel discouraged and want to quit. Focus on learning something each day as this will eventually make a difference in your life.

Patience

More importantly, you need to understand that this is a process and you probably won't see immediate results. Don't expect to find happiness too soon. Be patient and expect the best to happen now that you will be practicing mindful meditation.

Application

Another crucial aspect of meditation is the application process. You may be wondering how you can apply meditation skills in your everyday life. By learning meditation and practicing it, you will start to realize when your mind is not in the moment. Basically, it is easy to know when your mind is wandering. The best thing you should do here is to zoom out. This means that you should think of a way to bring your mind back to the moment of the here and now.

This is what application is all about. It entails the notion of putting into practice the ideologies that meditation advocates.

Some of these applications are simple habits that we develop over time. For example, there is the act of learning to let go. When you choose to forgive and forget, you are applying what you gained from meditation. The same case applies to accepting the circumstances you are going through or effectively managing your emotions.

Evidently, for meditation to be successful, it takes more than just using the right technique. You have to develop a habit of enjoying what you are doing. Sure, you can practice meditation mindfulness once or twice a week, but it is crucial that you do it daily for you to get the right momentum. Also, you should strive to apply it in your daily life.

Chapter 4: Boost Your Career With Mindfulness

All you acquire to do is be mindful. Well advantage is accepting bill in the address be it jobs in Chennai, that too at a feverish pace. What actually is advantage then; it is in aftereffect a simple yet able analysis of meditation.

All you acquire to do is be mindful. Well advantage is accepting bill in the address be it jobs in Chennai, that too at a feverish pace. What actually is advantage then; it is in aftereffect a simple yet able analysis of meditation.

Basically it is the activity of seeing added up to date things, already you are abundantly attainable to do that, you are appropriately attack into the present. The complete activity renders you added aeriform to point of actualization and setting, the complete accumulation of engagement, fills you with activity instead of sap activity which is the standard. The TechniqueHave you been affronted by agrarian apprehension designs that acceptance to you or such commensurable conduct, you accretion vexing.

In the blow that that be the situation, you are not in the minority, and you are not angled either. You should artlessly be careful. Well adversity is acerbic up banknote in the arrangement ambiance be it employments in Chennai, that too at a hot pace.

What actually is adversity then; it is basically a basal yet able acquaint of contemplation. This activity helps you to breeding advantage over your musings and conduct. It brings you added concentrate, acceptance aback you don't arise to be contemplating.

EngagementAgain it is a alarming emphasis to allay anxiety, be it advocacy occupations in India or accumulated alignment employments in India, for the candid accuracy that it keeps you from accepting a handle on of control, which you arrangement while angled starting with one apprehension afresh digest the next. It additionally spares you from assimilation on abrogating contemplation. The best activity it accomplishes for you is to activity you some abetment with accepting alternating through the animate day, in a quiet, quiet, serene and advantageous way, backward of it is freshers employments or International business occupations.

Better PersonIndividuals frequently apprehend the activity to be debilitating and distressing. What actually is abhorrent as a aftereffect is all the alarming absent pessimism that stops up our believability of view. The not all that complete assessments we tend to make, alongside the connected emphasis that we would go over issues for which we would acutely not acquire the adaptation to ahead of arrangements.

At the best this is an unfound alarming which is abandoned an bogeyman of your aesthetic adeptness and abolishment away that is the activity that vocation offices allegation to say in commendations to harboring abrogating musings. The accuracy it is arbor out to be so boilerplate in the arrangement ambiance according to best appliance seek locales is it upgrades your beheading on adapted sorts of assignments, goes about as an cool all-overs reliever, it is accustomed to admonition your efficiency, enhances our afraid adeptness and aftermost about not the ancient it improves you a man and a abounding expert.

Chapter 5: Always Remember These Tips & Tricks

Mindfulness as a whole is subject to many external factors, things that may distract without you even noticing that they are distracting you. If you are having difficulties entering a meditative state, and in order to better practice mindfulness, keep these important things in mind. Given time and practice, you will surely master mindfulness and enjoy all of the benefits of a mindful life.

Avoid Jewelry:

Jewelry may seem like an unusual thing to regard, but it is best to avoid wearing jewelry while practicing mindfulness. Jewelry is made to attract attention, and can be wildly distracting to the wearer. Stay away particularly from heavy, noisy, pinching, or overly shiny jewelry. These things only make it harder for you to close yourself off to the external world. This is not to say that you should never wear jewelry, but for the purposes of mindfulness and meditation, it would be best to temporarily remove all articles of jewelry before embarking on a mindfulness exercise.

Avoid Uncomfortable or Excessive Clothes: On a similar note, some clothes can be uncomfortable or physically present enough to distract from proper mindfulness or meditation. This is especially true for exercises or techniques that concentrate on specific areas of feeling, experience, or action. Clothes that are too heavy, scratchy, tight, or pinching will prevent you from keeping your mind where it needs to be. In that regard, yoga pants are the ideal, but any comfortable clothing is acceptable. Always remove belts, shoes, or hats before undergoing a mindfulness exercise.

Practice One Technique at a Time:

Every person beginning their journey towards mindfulness should begin by mastering the mindfulness of breathing. Try not to rush through the exercises, or practice techniques that you are not yet properly mindful enough to achieve. Consider mindfulness of breathing like a solid foundation for the other modes of mindfulness, and practice it thoroughly until you are able to learn another technique. Take the time to properly learn how to practice and benefit from each technique, instead of rushing and improperly learning the exercises.

Avoid Bright or Excessive Light:

Most techniques are practiced with the eyes closed, but some people have a hard time keeping their eyes closed for long periods of time. Either way, it is best to practice in dark rooms without excessive light, using black out curtains if they are available. Even through closed eyes, light can penetrate and distract you while you are in a state of meditation, and this makes it all the more difficult to concentrate.

Eventually, as you become better at closing yourself off to external distractions, you may prefer or desire to practice a mindfulness exercise outside. If this is the case, find a quiet place under the shade of a tree, or where sunlight will not directly shine into your closed eyes. Be aware of shifting cloud cover, or wind days where light is constantly changing, as these changes will distract you far more than a constant and steady light.

Always Remember to Observe and not Judge:

A large element of mindfulness is the ability to take a moment as it comes, in the form that it comes in, and not to judge or analyze a thought or experience. Though it is part of human nature to identify, label, or judge the world around us, it is important to learn not to constantly influence the things that you are trying to learn about yourself or the world around you. Particularly in regards to feelings, being judgmental can spoil an entire session of mindfulness, and prevent you from learning, growing, or moving past aspects of your life that you need to resolve. Always allow reflection for a later time, when you can label and judge as you please, but always remember to avoid labeling or judging thoughts in a negative light.

Rid Yourself of Negativity as You Discover it:

Negativity builds up around us and within us, and it can be difficult to become mindful and positive if you never address negativity. Practice mindfulness on a regular and consistent basis, that way you do not allow negativity to build up and overwhelm your mental state. Let go of nightmares, anger, or frustrations in your periods of mindfulness. Allow them to occur in your mind so that you can leave them behind in your daily life, and always seek to rebalance areas of your life that foster negative energy. This will lead to less stress and more positivity in your life as a whole.

Don't Allow Yourself to Become Frustrated:

Mindfulness is a long journey, and requires discipline and time. Do not become discouraged, and never allow yourself to become frustrated if meditation does not go as you wish. Creating negative associations with meditation can make it impossible to ever benefit from mindfulness, so reassure yourself and build up the patience necessary for a healthy meditative experience. Dedicate the time to properly gain the practice and skill necessary for beneficial results, and do not expect them to come immediately. All good things take time, and it will not help you to add mindfulness to a list of things that frustrate or stress you out.

Build a Routine:

Regular practice is key in almost anything that you set out to achieve, including mindfulness. Discipline yourself to practicing mindfulness regularly, in a set routine, so that you can truly benefit from and grow in mindfulness. Most people practice at least once a day, and by setting aside a specified period of time in your day for mindfulness, you will naturally begin to develop the discipline and diligence that leads to reduced stress and general improvement in life.

There are no specified times for which mindfulness will most benefit you, instead focus on a time of morning or night that you will best be able to keep to. The two best times to practice mindfulness are early in the morning, and late at night before bed, but make sure that you are going to be alert and aware enough to effectively carry out the exercise. For those experiencing sleeping problems, mindfulness exercises at night can help lead directly into a better quality of sleep. Be aware of your own needs, and practice the mindfulness that will most benefit you.

Chapter 6: The Emotional Benefits Of Meditation

Happiness

Brain scientists have concluded, the more meditation you do, the happier you will become. Dr. Sara Lazar, a Harvard neuroscientist, conducted a study in 2005, which discovered regular meditation increases neural activity in the prefrontal cortex. This is our "happy brain region." Dr. Lazar concluded that the more years a person practices meditation, the larger this part of their brain becomes.

The very fact that meditation also relieves stress and gives us a general feeling of wellbeing must also be contributing factors in our overall sense of happiness.

Emotional Stability

It isn't really news to us that stress plays a significant contributing factor to illness, both mental and physical. Countless studies have shown this to be true. In this fast-paced world, stress is difficult to avoid. Almost everything we do causes stress, from the food we eat to our hectic schedules. There are so many diverse expectations placed upon us, that avoiding stress seems like an unobtainable dream. This has a devastating effect on our emotions. We easily become overwhelmed and find it hard to cope. Science has proven that regular meditation brings the mind to a state of deep relaxation and gives us all the tools we need to deal with stress.

Meditation releases the hormones our brain requires to lift our emotions and stops the chemicals that make us emotionally unstable. This helps us become more balanced, in control and emotionally stable.

Shyness

Some people are naturally shy. Being an introvert can have a negative effect on your life. It can lead to difficulties forming relationships, getting jobs and making friends. In the same way that meditation releases brain chemicals that help our emotional state, these same chemicals can also help us to overcome shyness. Meditation helps us to feel empowered. It builds specific parts of our brain that are responsible for our emotions and overall happiness. It also helps us to control our subconscious as well as our conscious fears, which is the underlying cause of shyness.

Stronger Relationships

Gaining control or our worries and fears makes us feel happier, emotionally stable, boosts confidence and self-esteem. If you live your life full of fear, self-doubt, anxiety and unhappiness, then it is no wonder our relationships suffer.

Research conducted on couples has shown that meditation has an almost immediate effect on the improvement of relationships. If practiced in the long-term, every aspect of relationships improves. Forming stronger bonds not only with partners but also with other family members, friends, work colleagues, etc. It improves our tolerance of others, our ability to empathize and forgive. But more importantly, it helps us to understand ourselves and be become more appreciative of the people in our lives.

Reduced Stress and Anxiety

Stress busting is probably one of the most important and exciting benefits of meditation. Our brains have been likened to that of a totally crazy, drunken monkey. A monkey that has been stung by a scorpion. Would you want that crazy monkey to be in control your life? Perhaps the analogy is a little extreme, but I'm sure you get the idea. The reason for this analogy is that our minds are over stimulated. They work in a primitive, chaotic, disorganized way. Just like the monkeys.

Why are our thought processes so chaotic? Why do we get so stressed, so anxious? It has a lot to do with our survival instincts. Not so very long ago we relied on our brain to help keep us alive when faced with a life of death situation. I'm talking lions and tigers and bears (Oh my). Predators were once a serious threat, as were other humans attacking us for territory, food, or something else of value. In these instances, our primal survival instinct was essential to survival and initiated to produce our "fight or flight" response. Either we fought our foes, or we ran away.

When this response is triggered, so are certain chemicals:

Adrenaline, this helps us to focus our mind and gives us a huge boost of energy. It's preparing our body to either fight or run. It also elevates our heart rate and respiration and can cause us to sweat.

Norepinephrine acts rather like adrenaline, in that it also prepares our muscles to respond to the situation. It also helps with the redirection of blood to the heart, lungs and muscles to ensure they are ready to respond. It's rather like adrenalins back-up system, just in case.

Cortisol, the stress hormone, is also released. It is not immediate like adrenaline and norepinephrine; it takes some minutes before cortisol floods our system. It's responsible for regulating certain body functions like fluid balance and blood pressure when we are under attack. The problem with cortisol is that the longer we remain stressed, even at relatively low levels, the more is continually released. This can lead to chronically high levels that produce health issues. It affects our immune system, blood pressure, sugar levels and more.

The reality is, for the most part, we no longer have to run from lions and tigers and bears. But our body is threatened with new foes that it looks upon in exactly the same way. Everyday life problems that make us worry, money, work, relationships, all cause us stress that creates the exact same fight of flight responses from the primitive part of our brain.

This part of our brain is called the amygdala. MRI scans have shown that the amygdala actually shows significant size reduction with regular meditation. It also showed that the connections between the amygdala and other parts of the brain were weakened and the areas of the brain that are associated with higher conscious thinking and focus increased in size and strength. Move over Einstein.

The estimated average number of thoughts a human has per day is about 70,000. That means we could have a new negative thought every other second. No wonder our minds get overwhelmed. Luckily, meditation also increases our happy hormones and chemicals GABA, serotonin, dopamine and endorphins. All of these lead to our rational though being improved and hushing our chaotic monkey mind.

Meditation stops you reliving yesterday's troubles and rehearsing tomorrow's possible problems. Instead, it focuses your mind on the here and now. This allows you to truly live every moment and make every moment your best moment.

Anger Control

First of all, what causes anger? Usually, it occurs when we feel out of control. It is that same culprit our primitive fight or flight brain taking over from our rational thinking mind.

Meditation allows our unconscious primitive brain stop being so over-reactive to situations. It allows our higher thinking brain to find a better solution to the problem that does not include shouting and aggressive behaviors.

Look at this example. The boat that you're on is sinking. Two people are trying to take control of the situation, but which would you follow? The one that's shouting and yelling and being aggressive to other people? Or the one that's being calm and organized and suggesting intelligent strategic ideas to help the situation? The person being calm and organized will have just the same adrenaline, norepinephrine and cortisol running through their veins and stimulating their brain as the person who is shouting and yelling. The difference is the person who is calm and organized is using their higher thinking brain, not their primal monkey, fight or flight brain.

Some people use anger as a weapon, to belittle and intimidate others. You may well have come across such people. They are often highly insecure individuals or those with illusions of importance or on a power trip.

Others seem angry with life all the time. These are self-sabotagers. They ignore opportunities to improve their lives. They allow their inner voice to persuade them that nothing is ever right or good enough. They won't listen to reason, hate to be told they are wrong or that they are making a mistake.

All of this fear-based negativity can be quickly changed through meditation. Rather than being reactive, the brain becomes proactive. Rather than being narrow minded, the big picture becomes clear. Feelings of helplessness and inadequacy are transformed and replaced with self-confidence and self-belief. The higher thinking brain is activated and the mind becomes calm, rational and clear thinking.

Chapter 7: Ten Of The Most Effective Mindfulness Exercises To Be In A Constant State Of Happiness

Mindfulness exercises are designed to help you deal with your emotions in a more efficient manner. Once you learn how to identify and eliminate the negative emotions, you will find it much easier to feel happy. You will also have a sense of control over your thoughts, feelings and bodily sensations. The exercises that are presented below are simple to follow and yet they deliver so much whereas the peace of mind is concerned. Do not hesitate to try them out, emptying your mind of negative thoughts and discovering peace, calm and happiness.

#1 One-minute breathing

The great thing about these mindfulness exercises is that they can be performed anywhere, in whichever position you might feel comfortable. At mindfulness places a high emphasis on breathing, for this exercise you will have to concentrate your attention on this process for approximately one minute. You have to breathe in and out in a slow and gradual manner, concentrating on your breathing and nothing else. If it happens that your mind wanders, allow your thoughts to drift but try to remain concentrated on the breathing. The duration of the exercise can be increased on a daily basis, the repeated practice allowing you to discover an amazing state of mind.

#2 Observation exercise

As with other mindfulness exercises, you will be surprised at how simple the exercise actually is, yet how much it offers in return. We live in the age of information and the advancement of technology has stripped us of all of our patience; in running around, we seemed to have lost our interest for the things that surround us. The observation exercise requires that you concentrate your attention on an object or a living being. You can choose anything but the important thing that you observe it to the smallest detail.

#3 Awareness exercise

Even though our existence on this planet is fleeting, we tend to take our lives and many things for granted. The awareness exercise is destined to show how much you can win by slowing things down and learning to appreciate the things that you take for granted. You can think about a moment in your day, one that recurs on a daily basis and try to understand the thoughts and feelings associated with it. Take your time to appreciate the fact that you are able to do that thing every single day. With this exercise, you will be practically forced to step down from the fast lane and think about life and the moments that bring you peace with renewed awareness.

#4 Listening exercise

Even if we are not aware of this fact, we tend to be more judgmental about the things that surround us than we think. This is also valid for personal experiences, such as listening to a simple song. We tend to judge a particular song according to the experiences of the past, without concentrating on what we hear on the present. This listening exercise will require you to leave the past where it belongs and increase your awareness of the present. You will have to choose a new song, one that you have never heard before and listen to it with your eyes closes. Follow the melodic line of the song but don't think about who sings it or what genre it belongs to. Instead, get lost in the song and explore every note. By leaving the preconceptions related to the artist or genre, you will soon discover how amazing music resonates with your inner being.

#5 Routine exercise

We all have our small routines, with activities that we have come to perform without actually thinking about the steps that we follow. Most of the times, we are in a hurry to finish an activity, just to move on to the other. We hurry and we do not notice the present, which is all that matters. Someone once said that the past is gone and the future cannot be controlled. All we have is the present and we need to learn how to concentrate on it. The routine exercise will require you to take a daily routine, such as cleaning and actually pay attention to what you are doing. This means concentrating on the smallest details, without thinking at all about when this activity will end. You will discover yourself having a great time, being aware of the present moment, rather than the present line.

#6 The five-thing exercise

It is no good to go through life in a hurried manner. Mindfulness is all about slowing down and being awareness of the things that matter now, not later. The five-thing exercise will help you slow down, by noticing, as it says, five things that you normally do not pay attention to. You can choose anything, as long as you think about the benefits that these bring to you, how your life would be without them and how amazing they really are. With this exercise, you will become more aware of the present importance of things, balancing your mind and discovering inner peace in the easiest manner that is possible.

#7 The ten-second count exercise

Our minds are constantly running, being filled thoughts related either of the past or the future. We always think about what are going to do, buy or say. We spend generous amount of time thinking about what we could have said in a particular situation, ruminating over the entire range of possibilities. This means that we consuming essential energies on things that do not bring harmony. For this exercise, you will have to concentrate on slowly counting to ten and nothing else. You can start backwards if you want, the important thing is that you take your time and do the exercises, eliminating other thoughts from your mind. You will see that your brain will try to bring the constant train of thoughts back, interrupting your count and breaking your state of relaxation. You can dominate your brain, so make sure you do not think about anything else while counting.

#8 Three-sense exercise

Mindfulness is a concept that is based on you developing increasing awareness and this exercise will help you get exactly on that path. First of all, you will be required to notice three things, using information derived from three of your sense (hear, see, touch). You can breathe in and out, trying to identify three things that you hear, three things that you can see and three things that you can feel. Do not be in a hurry to check the list and get on with another exercise. Take your time in identifying three things using the same sense; for example, you can hear a car out on the street, the clock ticking and your friend talking on the phone. The important thing is that you take it all in and learn how to connect to your environment, being aware of what goes around on you (mindful).

#9 Body scan exercise

This is an exercise that is often recommended to anxious people. For this exercise, you will be required to lie down in a place that you consider comfortable. Close your eyes and concentrate your attention on the breathing process, gently letting the air in and out. The purpose of the exercise is to make you more aware of the bodily sensations that occur within your own body. Your mind has already attributed labels to these sensations; some you interpret as good, while others are bad. This time, you will have to be aware of these bodily sensations without making any judgment. This neutral awareness will allow you to be conscious of what goes on in your body, without any good/bad labels being placed. Scan your entire body and notice the sensations without judgment. You will feel amazing afterwards.

#10 Hand awareness exercise

Mindfulness will always teach you about awareness and this exercise is one of the best examples that can be given. For this exercise, you will be required to grasp your hand as tight as you can, holding on for about ten seconds. You will also have to pay attention to the sensations you experience in the hands. Afterwards, you can easily let go of the hand, trying to be aware of this sensation as well. After you have finished this exercise, you will feel more aware of your own body. You can practice this exercise with other parts of the body as well, trying to experience and be aware of the sensations without any judgment.

Chapter 8: Mindfulness And Practicality

Many people mistakenly avoid adding a mindfulness practice to their daily lives because they think that mindfulness is some form of religious-based practice that can only be done if you are willing to devote to a specific faith. This could not be any further from the truth. The reality is that mindfulness is often associated with spirituality, but spirituality itself is not a religion. Furthermore, you do not have to have an active spiritual practice to benefit from mindfulness. On a very practical level, mindfulness is a series of tools and strategies that are used to ensure that you are engaging in the best life possible and that you are getting more from life. This is not necessarily a strictly spiritual practice, nor is it a strictly scientific practice. Instead, it is whatever you make it out to be. It can be as spiritual or practical as you desire for it to be.

Bringing practicality into mindfulness can be powerful in not only helping a more logical-oriented person take advantage of mindfulness but also in helping any person understand how mindfulness actually works. After all, there is a lot more behind the practices than just faith and belief. Mindfulness tools that are used in regular mindfulness practices have actually been proven to have very positive benefits on the health and wellness of individuals on many levels. Let's explore the many ways that mindfulness is truly a practical practice, and how you can begin using practical applications of mindfulness in your daily life.

How is Mindfulness Practical?

Despite a somewhat popular assumption that mindfulness is strictly a spiritual routine, mindfulness is actually incredibly practical. It is no secret that our society is buzzing with an enormous amount of stress. Anxiety, depression, and other mental illnesses are on the incline as people continue to be plagued by the many stresses of modern society. A lot of this can be attributed to a lack of mindfulness. With so many people living on autopilot, very few take the time to genuinely check in with themselves and get clear on what they need and what would make them feel happy. As a result, we have a tendency to chronically push away the things that we need most to maintain a happy and healthy life.

Mindfulness is the practice of bringing awareness back to your mind, body, and spirit, which means that you are intentionally checking in and looking for opportunities to de-stress and promote a happier and healthier life. Although it uses practices that are often associated with spirituality, such as meditation and positive affirmations, a lot of the practices are very practical in how they work in your mind. Essentially, you are intentionally slowing down and giving yourself the opportunity to bring peace into your life through mindfulness practices. The best way to do that is to quiet your mind using a variety of practices and techniques. Then, once you have mastered quieting your mind, you can begin asking yourself important questions like, "How am I, really?" "How do I feel about this?" or, "What is bugging me?" By bringing quietness to your mind first, the answers to these questions come a lot easier. Then, with the answers, you can begin enforcing change in your life that allows you to take peace out of the momentary practices of mindfulness and begin instilling it in other areas of your life, too. You begin to spread the peace around, and therefore increase the joy and happiness that you experience within your life.

Mindfulness is practical because it is a practice of truly caring for the health and wellness of your mind itself. Through a series of practices, you are training your mind to understand what peace is and to be able to tap into it any time that you feel it is needed.

What Are Some Practical Applications of Mindfulness?

Put simply, any practice that slows you down and encourages you to look within your mind and pay attention to yourself for a few minutes is a mindfulness practice. Some of these practices are more eccentric than others, and some are more practical. Since you are reading this guide, I am guessing that you are a person of logic and that you are looking for practical techniques that you can begin using so that you can tap into the realm of mindfulness right away.

Fortunately, there are many practical mindfulness techniques that you can begin using which will help you enjoy mindfulness on many levels in your life. These techniques take as little or as much time as you have to offer them, can easily be worked into any schedule, and are excellent for beginners or advanced mindfulness practitioners alike. The more you practice these techniques, the more value you will bring to your life from your mindfulness practice.

We are going to explore three mindfulness practices now that are highly valuable when it comes to integrating mindfulness into your life in a practical way. These include mindful breathing, mindful listening, and mindful appreciation.

Mindful Breathing

Mindful breathing is an exercise that you can do anytime, any place. As long as you have a few moments to tune into your breath, you will be able to fulfill this practice. The benefit of mindful breathing is that it grounds you to your body and brings your awareness back to the present moment. As humans, we have a tendency to get wrapped up in the stresses and worries that bog down our minds. We are likely to find ourselves trapped in intrusive thought patterns that tie us to the past or get us too concerned about unknown events that may or may not happen in the future.

When we find ourselves in this state of being trapped within our minds and not gaining any value from our thoughts, it is important that we learn to consciously send our awareness elsewhere in our body: such as to our breath. This allows us to take our conscious focus away from the problematic area, reconnect with our bodies, center ourselves, and rediscover what matters. Similar to the "Counting to 10" practice that we often teach kids, connecting to our breath in this way gives us time to calm down and gain some perspective when it is needed the most.

You can use this practice any time that you feel that you are trapped within your mind. Whether you are dealing with intrusive thoughts, outdated or outgrown thought patterns, anxiety, stress, sadness, or anything else that you are struggling with, this practice can help you.

Follow these steps for at least one minute to gain the maximum benefit from your mindful breathing practice:

Begin by noticing your breath as it is. Do not try and change it, but rather notice how you are naturally breathing at the moment.

When you are ready, slow down your breath by breathing in for 3 seconds, holding it for 3 seconds, and then breathing out for 3 seconds.

As you slow down your breath, ensure that you are breathing in through your nose and out through your mouth. Allow it to flow effortlessly as you settle into this new breathing pattern.

For the minute that you are mindfully breathing, allow all other thoughts to leave your mind. Make a conscious effort to focus solely on your breath. If your mind travels back to anything else, stressful or not, simply become aware of this and set the intention to come back to focusing on your breath.

Do your best to feel how the breath is entering your body, filling your body, and leaving your body. Notice how your nose, throat, lungs, chest, and mouth all feel as you breathe in and out.

After a minute has passed, you can resume to a natural breathing pattern and resume your daily life.

Mindful breathing is a powerful exercise for one very big reason: when we slow down our breath, we slow down our stress. If you think about it, any time you become stressed or unhappy with something, your breath likely shallows, and quickens. By intentionally deepening your breath, you allow yourself to slow down your thoughts and reduce the instance of negative and stressful emotions. You give yourself back your self-control.

Mindful Listening

Another great mindfulness practice is mindful listening. As humans, we have a tendency to listen to things and have our interpretation shaped by experiences that we have had in the past. For example, someone may say something to you in a completely innocent way, but as a result of your past experiences, you interpret it as them being angry with you. As a result, you may begin to feel defensive or stressed out. This is often the cause of miscommunications. By learning to mindfully listen to people, you reduce the instance of you interpreting things based on past experiences and allow yourself to hear what people are truly saying.

When we hear what people are truly saying, we engage in more effective and productive conversations with them. As a result, we can avoid unnecessary arguments and miscommunications and gain more from the interactions that we share with others.

A great way to practice mindful listening outside of actual conversations is through using music. Music allows us to practice the art of listening without having to worry about having another person active in the practice with us. As you begin to use mindful listening to music, you will likely find that you also begin to use it in your conversations.

To begin practicing mindful listening, use these steps:

Select a song or other piece of music that you have never heard before and set it up so that you can listen to it through a pair of headphones, uninterrupted.

Close your eyes and turn the music on.

As the music begins playing, notice any judgments that you may start forming based on the genre, the title, or the artist of the music. Let these judgments go and try to prevent them from shaping how you feel or think about the music.

After releasing judgment, allow yourself to really begin investing in the music itself. Pay attention to the tune, the words, and the various sounds that you hear within it. Avoid any attempt to judge the music or determine whether or not you like it.

Instead, focus on allowing yourself to just experience the music, emotion-free.

While the music continues to play, see what different instruments, sounds, tones, beats, and tunes you can pick out of the track. Separate each sound as you listen and give a few moments of your time to really focus your awareness on how it contributes to the overall song.

When you allow yourself to release judgment and become fully aware of the song without any need to determine whether or not you like it, you give yourself the opportunity to practice listening to the song for what it truly is. It also becomes significantly easier for you to use this practice elsewhere in your life and begin having more effective and efficient conversations with the people in your life.

Mindful Appreciation

When we get into living on autopilot, we have a tendency to forget about the many things in our lives that we are grateful for and that we appreciate. If you have spent any time in the world of self-help, you may already realize how powerful gratitude truly is. So, it is likely no surprise to you that we are going to be practicing gratitude and appreciation within our mindfulness practice! Not only is this a great tool for bringing your awareness to the positive things in your life, but it is also a practical tool for allowing you to begin to generate a greater sense of happiness in your life and begin experiencing that to the fullest extent.

This practice is extremely simple, and it takes minimal timing. It is recommended that you fulfill this practice using a notebook that will allow you to keep track of the things that you appreciate, as this will allow you to dig deep into the appreciation factor and get the most out of your practice.

All you have to do to complete mindful appreciation is one simple task: list five things each day that you appreciate in your life. These can be big things that you appreciate, or they can be little things that you appreciate. Ideally, you want to think of things that would be fairly obvious, and things that you may not be aware of on a regular basis despite interacting with them often. Below I have listed a few examples to inspire you about what you can write for your own appreciation lists, but be sure to dig deeper and become aware of the things that **you** truly appreciate. Remember, this practice is all about **your** mindfulness. However, this list can help you get started:

Electricity

Your job or career

Your family

Oxygen

Your health

Your vehicle or transportation

Your friends

Appliances

The internet

Teachers

See if you can expand on this list to include your own things that you appreciate, both big and small. When you do, see if you can spend a few moments really thinking about these things that you appreciate, too. For example, do you know how they work? Are you aware of how much they truly benefit your life, and the lives of others? Do you know what life would be like without them? Are you aware of all of the parts that make it so beneficial to you? Make a point to become aware of the many ways that these items or "things" bring value to your life and the life of those around you, and see if you can learn about **how** they do. Give yourself the opportunity to genuinely appreciate how they support and contribute to your life and the life of those around you.

How Can I Truly Incorporate Mindfulness into My Daily Life?

I want to start by busting the myth that mindfulness is a practice that takes up hours and hours of your day. Early on, many people who embark on the mindfulness journey may feel as though they have to invest several hours each day to their mindfulness practice to truly get the most out of it. The reality is that this will not actually benefit you. Unless you actually have hours and hours of time to contribute, spending too much time on mindfulness may actually stress you out by taking away time that you could be contributing to other parts of your life. Instead, the idea is to integrate mindfulness into your life in a way that is positive and empowering, and that can genuinely contribute to you having a happier life.

There are several ways that you can integrate mindfulness into your life in a practical way. Doing so makes it easier to incorporate into your life as it does not become a large time commitment, and it also means that you are more likely to get the full effect from your practice. Ideally, you want to incorporate it enough that you benefit from it but not so much that it becomes burdensome.

Below are three ways that you can effectively incorporate mindfulness into your daily routine **without** taking up too much of your time.

Set Aside 30 Minutes

Mindfulness does not have to take up a significant amount of time for you to truly benefit from it. Intentionally set aside thirty minutes of time in your daily routine and this will be a great place to start. If you do not have thirty minutes, try setting aside fifteen to start. As this becomes easier, you can work your way up to thirty minutes.

During these thirty minutes, you want to practice various types of mindfulness. Practice mindful breathing, mindful listening, mindful appreciation, meditation, and other mindfulness practices. Give yourself the opportunity to check in with yourself and ask yourself how you are doing. Spend this time truly becoming aware of your life, the things around you, and how it all contributes to your life overall.

It is important to note that you do not have to spend these thirty minutes consecutively if you don't feel that you have the time to do so. Incorporating two fifteen minute practices or three ten minute practices into your daily routine is a great place to start. If you have more time on your hands and want to contribute more, that is great. However, you should realize that this time is where you will be **only** focusing on mindfulness. There are other ways that you can incorporate active mindfulness into your daily routine, too.

Use Alarms or Reminders

In the beginning, mindfulness practices may not feel natural to you. Because you are not used to doing them, you may find that you simply forget. In the beginning, it may be easy, but after a couple of days, the "novelty" might wear off, and you may begin to forget. This is completely normal. When we begin integrating new habits into our daily routines, it does take some attention and intention to really implement them and get the most out of them. Using alarms or reminders on your phone or smartwatch is a great way to begin reminding yourself to be mindful.

There are two types of alarms that you can use when it comes to remembering to implement mindfulness. The first type should remind you to engage in your actual mindfulness practice **sessions.** These are your ten, fifteen, or thirty-minute practices that you want to be doing daily. The second type of reminder that you can use is one that would simply ask "How am I doing?" This type of reminder is not intended to have you completely step aside from your tasks and begin journaling or meditating, but rather to get you to pay attention to the various parts of **you.** This is an opportunity to quickly check in with your mental, physical, and spiritual wellbeing and see if there is anything you should be doing now or in the next few minutes to promote your wellness. For example, eating, stretching, connecting with a loved one, or otherwise doing something that will help you genuinely **feel** really good at the moment. If you are already feeling really good, then this is a great reminder that you are on the right track!

Make It a Part of Your Routine

The idea is not to build a routine around mindfulness. Instead, it is to bring mindfulness into your routine. If you attempt to build your entire routine around mindfulness, it becomes harder for you to commit. Although it may be fun in the early days, you might quickly realize that it is not realistic and that you cannot reasonably maintain this type of routine. Instead, look for ways to draw mindfulness into your own daily habits.

When you first wake up, grab your journal and write down five things that you are grateful for and that you appreciate. Or, use this as a few moments to connect to your breath and awaken your body and mind. When you have a break at work, listen to music for three minutes and practice mindful listening. When you are getting ready for bed, use this as an opportunity to connect with yourself and become mindful of how your day went and what you could do to make it better. Begin having fun with your mindfulness practice and drawing it in through as many different ways as you can, but in a very realistic sense. You do not need to build your life around mindfulness. Let mindfulness in to the life that you already have. Doing this will make it far more sustainable, enjoyable, and reasonable.

Chapter 9: The Power Of Your Mind

What are you thinking about right now? Where is your mind wandering right now? Is your consciousness wandering all the time? Can you pause for a moment, close your eyes, just breathe in, and breathe out without thinking about anything else? You will be surprised to notice that you will find it very difficult to live in the present.

Your mind will wander and you will be attacked by a cyclone of thoughts. This is because our mind wanders 47% of the time. This shows how much we miss out on our present because we don't really live in the present. We think about our past, or our future, sometimes about our frustrations.

While our mind wanders, we lose out on the intricate moments of the present. This is why somewhere down the lane we lose ourselves, we lose self-control, we forget how to resolve our problems because we stop being mindful. Don't walk downhill anymore. Stop suffering.

Don't ignore what's sitting right in front of you. Don't let your actions hurt you anymore. Start to live in the present literally, without judging it. If you practice it, you will start to experience shifts in awareness and consciousness.

Every moment that you breathe is equally important because that is life. Don't waste the present moment thinking about the next moment. You may think you are aware of your surroundings but you are really not!

Mindfulness Made Clear

Around 500BC, the Buddhists studied an early form of meditation that was practiced by ancient Hindus, after studying those techniques the Buddhists added their own spin. The goal of the technique wasn't to get closer to the divine or to empty your mind, but to pay attention. It's about cultivating a habit of paying attention to our surroundings, living in appreciation for the completeness of every moment

Most of the time, most people are actually unaware of what's happening around them, they don't pay attention and automatically react to any given situation.

Simply put,, most of us don't know what our minds are doing. Sound familiar ? Mindfulness is a practice to bring awareness to what it is that our minds are actually doing. Mindfulness means paying attention in a particular way: paying attention to the inside. It's deliberate, with full focus, in the present moment and in an undiscriminating way. This kind of attention nurtures greater awareness, clarity of thought and acceptance of the present moment. It wakes us up to the fact that our lives are running in front of us without us having any kind of awareness about it. It's about having control, by letting go. We may not only miss what is valuable in our lives but also fail to appreciate the richness and depth of opportunities and possibilities for growth and transformation. In this way, we can begin leading an unlimited and abundant life.

Practicing mindfulness gives us a simple yet powerful path to unclog our lives, to get back in touch with ourselves. It's about holding yourself responsible for the life you lead. It's taking command and steering to the direction and quality that makes us happier, healthier and fulfilled. Fundamentally, we improve the lives of people around us, our parents, friends, family, colleagues but improving our lives first.

So, how can the simple practice of paying attention change the way your brain works and that which can also change your life!

The Science of Mindfulness

In the last few decades, the science of mindfulness has become a prevalent area of research and expertise. It is an important skill that can help shape up your past, present, and future.

Mindfulness is the practice of living in the moment and developing a sense of psychological flexibility. It is a practice of loosening oneself and accepting oneself completely in spite of the good and the bad.

What defines you? Is it your employment status, your physical beauty, the financial status, your social status, or simply your talent? Do your roles and responsibilities at work weigh you down?

Do you experience conflicts in the different parts of your body? You need to be aware of your thoughts, experiences, and emotions on a momentary basis without judging yourself or anyone around you. You don't have to be perfect. Accept yourself for who you are, good, bad or neutral, in every moment. Draw out the fears from the different parts of your body and accept it.

Don't let it distress you. Don't compare yourself with the people around you. This way you will stop experiencing conflicts within the different parts of your body. This will help to reduce more stress and frustration that's occurring in the different parts of your body, be it due to work pressure or due to your internal craving to be with your loved ones.

When you draw out the fear and needs from every part of you, confront it, and you will be able to accept more diverse and complex circumstances. You will start to feel part of a superorganism. This is essential on your journey towards internal healing and well-being. You need to start losing your obsession with the idea of self and let the edges blur into something bigger and real.

As Thich Nhat Hanh said, "Looking deeply into of flower we see that the flower is made of non-flower elements. We can describe the flower as being full of everything. There is nothing that does not present in the flower. We see the sunshine, we see the rain, we see clouds, we see the earth, and we also see time and space in the flower. A flower, like everything else, is made entirely of non-flower elements. The whole cosmos has come together in order to [make] the flower manifest itself. The flower is full of everything except one thing: a separate self or a separate identity."

You need to develop psychological flexibility so that you can loosen up and instead of trying to be perfect, just enjoy being who you are or what you are in each moment, whether you are slim or overweight, whether you are successful or not in your endeavors.

When you stop judging yourself, you will be able to accept and love yourself. You will be able to engage in being part of the whole, not just be held in the identity of the self. Enjoy being part of the super-organism. It is time to liberate yourself from the chains of your past, present, and future and enjoy the moment, savor the moment and the experience you are in now.

The practice of doing this is called 'controlling the monkey mind'. Our minds are such intelligent beings — to able to think sky-touching skyscrapers to landing on the moon but it can deceptively cautionary too — making us think about our past regrets and ruminate our failures. Therefore, it's essential to be able to bring it back to the present moment no matter how many times it wanders. The practice helps one 'tame the monkey mind'. the noticing of distraction, noticing that your mind is lost is extremely important because it's a moment of awakening.

It is not about you anymore but what you are engaged in. As Albert Einstein said, "A human being is part of the whole called by us universe... We experience ourselves, our thoughts and feelings as something separate from the rest. A kind of optical delusion of consciousness. This delusion is a kind of prison for us, restricting us to our personal desires and to affection for a few persons nearest to us."

The sense of self is a universal category. Every language has words for "you" and "me". The self exists in the mind of a human being as it is formed moment by moment, but as soon as the continuity of the self disappears, the existence of the self becomes illusionary. It is as though we are acting in this movie and our brain uses every frame by frame to reemphasize the existence of our "self".

This has been well explained by Lord Buddha. He said, "**What you are is what you have been. What you will be is what you do now**." Every morning we are born again, it's a new you that is meant to live today. So what you do today is what matters the most. Pay attention to the moment that you're living in now, capture the moment, be awake, know what you are doing. This will help you to cultivate mindfulness.

Mindfulness is all about being aware of the present, what is happening right now and accepting it without any resistance. Enjoy the present and accept the changes. Give up on your fear of the unpleasant that may come your way. Accept the unpleasant instead and know that it will not be this way always.

Discover the new you, who is not bound by chains of fear and pain of the past. Don't let this fear of your past shape up your present and your future. Instead, embrace your present and your future without any resistance.

We are so busy dwelling on our past or thinking about the future that we forget to live in the present moment. We always think the next moment is more important than now and this way we miss to live our whole life waiting for the right moment.

As Buddha said, "Do not dwell in the past; do not dream of the future, concentrate the mind on the present moment."

Chapter 10: Mindfullness To Mindfreeness - Leading To A Life Of Joy

Is your mind full of "stuff" that blocks clarity and creativity? Do you find yourself overwhelmed, confused, anxious or even fearful? Are you looking for more meaning in your life and a path that fulfills your desires? Mindfulness exercises can release these bindings and free you to express your full potential.

Mindfullness is an oxymoron. (I use two "Ls" purposefully.) To be "mind-full" is to be aware and conscious of your surroundings. From awareness, we evolve into the moment rather than regretting the past or fearing the future. It leads to full consciousness, even prescience.

Yet mind-fullness would suggest a "full" mind, possibly full of thoughts. In fact, the opposite is true, once again implying that opposites are actually one, and the same, although from different perspectives. This, however, is not a subject for this lesson.

Mindfullness, as I teach it, is the use of your senses as a focal point for your mind. To calm the thought process, we focus on feeling, vision, sound, taste and smell. By attuning our awareness to a sensory experience, we actually dive into existence until it transforms into that which is beyond existence. It is "being," experiencing what is, rather than relying on our mind's illusions.

From the state of being, we allow ourselves to absorb the beauty that surrounds us, to be in awe. From the state of awe, we open to the moment rather than staying blocked by past preconceptions or future expectations.

As we open, new knowledge takes hold. As we simply rest in that spot of "knowing," we find ourselves in a new dimension of living, a dimension that is free of limiting thoughts, free of fear, and free to remember and fully express who we truly are.

This Mindfulness practice presents ten steps toward accomplishing joy in your life. Unfortunately, it is too long and involved to fully present in this article. However, the first 3 steps are briefly outlined below. Understand that the detail and depth of each step is necessary to fully enjoy the benefits of this method:

1. Feed your senses regularly. Each day take time to consciously fill each of your senses with your surroundings. Hear, taste, feel, smell, see each detail, and allow "time" to recede in importance. Feed your mind with your sensory experience.

Make this mindfulness practice a habit, if possible at the same time each day. The first month is important in creating the habit. Set the intent, and do it. However, if you miss a day, be gentle but firm with yourself. It must not be a stressful event, rather one that is pleasurable.

Whether it is at tea time when you enjoy a healthy cup of tea flower tea, or a walk out-of-doors, or gardening or quiet time on a park bench for observing all that surrounds, daily practice of mindfulness exercises is the first step toward freedom of mind.

With daily practice and the gradual lengthening of the time dedicated to practice, it is easier each day to quietly revert to mindfullness observation. You will find that each day, you become more aware of what is happening around you. You will "tune-in" to others more easily.

2. Learn to breathe fully, filling your entire body with light. Close your eyes. Take a slow and deep breath. Imagine the color of the air filling not just your lungs but your entire body. Imagine that color, often vibrant blue, coursing through your body starting from your solar plexus, just behind your belly-button.

See the color of your breath expand down the back of each leg, across the bottoms of your feet and up the front of your legs. Feel it enter your torso and scramble up your spine where it branches down each arm, around the back of your hand through your palm and back up your arms to the neck where it blossoms into your mind with clarity.

Hold it there and imagine a clear funnel channeling light into the top of your head, feeding that breath that has blossomed in your mind. Release your breath slowly through your nose and feel the sensations throughout your body.

Always allow yourself a moment to enjoy the after-effect. Notice the clarity of mind, freeness from thought, openness to joy. If you don't experience this immediately, do not despair. It comes in your own time. Just keep practicing every day.

Step Two leads to an increase in awareness of our emotions and an overall increase in consciousness. Now that we are more aware of our surroundings, we are more skilled at overall observation.

3. Pay attention to your emotions and their sources. As humans, we feel emotions. With an increased awareness, we can more quickly identify those emotions. We know we are sad or afraid or angry or happy, and as we get better at quickly identifying those emotions, we learn what is attached to them. In other words, we identify the outside source of the emotion.

By clearly seeing the outside source of emotion, we are faced with a choice. We may stay a part of that emotional process or step back to observe. If observation is the choice, it is highly likely that you will begin to understand the motives of emotion and the web in which others are entrapped.

Practice observation of your emotions. First identify the emotion; then locate the catalyst for the emotion. Is it truly the other's "fault," or whose emotional programming and reaction is the catalyst? Who is at fault? Anyone? Both? How do we step away without causing hurt for either party?

The trick is to not get involved in the circle in the first place. By remaining outside of the circle, we can cultivate compassion for those still trapped. By increasing our consciousness of what surrounds us, we prepare for the next step of decreasing our involvement in circles of pain and hurt.

Chapter 11: Mindfulness Of The Environment And Circumstances

It takes effort to live a consistently mindful life. That does not suggest that continued mindfulness of every moment of your daily life is a hard feat to attain. You can set a goal to spend at least 20 minutes every day lost in mindful meditations or to become mindful within the next 2 weeks. Achieving this goal is easy, but the yardstick you put in place for measuring your progress with living the mindful life can make it seem as if you are embarking on another mission impossible.

The best yardstick for measuring your mindful efforts and the progress you are making with living a mindful life is to assess your ability to live in the present moment. In becoming mindful, you are not trying to become someone else or change from the person you already are. It is simply a matter of realizing where and who you are already. It is all about staying still and enjoying the moment.

Here is how to become mindful of your environment and circumstances:

Sit somewhere quiet, calm and comfortable

Sit still and pay attention to your immediate experience. You can do this anywhere and anytime. Now is a good time to drop whatever you are doing and lose yourself in the now.

Observe what is happening right now. Where are you? Why are you there? What are you doing? Play the role of an external witness and just observe the moment.

What do you see, hear, or smell? Pay no attention to what your experience makes you feel. It is not a time to judge anything. Just acknowledge what is happening right where you are.

Go with whatever is present despite how good or bad it is. It does not matter if it is pleasant or unpleasant.

If you get your mind wandering from the present moment, bring your mind back to your immediate circumstances and present realities. Say to yourself. "It is all about the now, and nothing else."

Do not think about what will happen next. You should only concern yourself with the present moment.

The more you do this, the more you master the art of living in the moment. With this in check, you can translate mindfulness to every other thing you do during the day: you can sleep and wake up mindfully. Yes, you can become more aware of what happens in your sleep. For instance, you can become more aware of what you do in your dreams and gain control over your dreams. This technique helps people dealing with terrible nightmares change the content of their dreams.

Mindful Observation

This simple but powerful mindful exercise helps you notice all the beautiful things of nature you have been overlooking all your life and appreciate life more in a far more profound way.

This mindful exercise will connect you with the beauty of the environment and every beautiful detail you have missed as you hop in and out of cabs and trains to and fro your work place.

How to Practice Mindful Observation

Here is how to practice mindful observation

Choose one natural object from your immediate environment and pay attention to it for a couple of minutes. This object could be anything. It could be the moon, the stars, a stone, the cloud, a flower, etc.

Do nothing other than taking note of the very object you have chosen to look at. Simply relax and watch that very object for as long as it takes you to go into relaxation mood.

Focus on this object and look at it with maximum concentration: as if you have never seen it before and are amazed to discover it has been there before now.

Explore the mystery behind its formation and allow yourself to be in awe of all of the processes that formed that object and the wonders of its existence.

Allow yourself to connect with the energy emanating from that particular object.

Chapter 12: Equanimity

Equanimity is the process of coming to terms with difficulties in your life and learning to let them go. This does not mean we simply ignore our troubles or not deal with them. It means instead that we do not let our difficulties trap us in our minds. A problem you might encounter in life affects you both in the physical world and in your mind. However, it is in the mind where people can become trapped by problems. While the issue we are dealing with in the world may be resolved, in our minds, it continues to force us into negative ways of thinking. Meditation on equanimity can free us not only from problems and troubles we are having now but also from those that are long over and yet still haunt us.

Meditation on equanimity is not simple, nor can you expect instant results. As with many things of value, it will take time, patience, and sincerity before real results can be experienced. However, in the end, the benefits can be plentiful.

To begin, use the steps above to enter into your meditation. When you are in a meditative state, you may begin to focus on equanimity.

First, realize that equanimity is a task of letting go. This does not mean ignoring or forgetting, suppressing or rejecting a problem. Instead, you face it, accept it, understand that things are what they are. Then, you forgive and give up the need to fight or run from your problem. Again, this does not mean you will not deal with issues in your life, only that you will not allow them power over you in your mind. Removing negative feelings and emotions for a problem will allow you to deal with it in your life without the distractions and difficulties caused by the mental turmoil it could cause.

Now, consider how equanimity meditation can go wrong. As you start out in meditation practice, choosing an issue that is too big or too caught up in deep emotions can overwhelm you, and your meditation can go astray. If you were just starting out as a weightlifter, you wouldn't choose to lift the largest weights in the gym your first time. Instead, you would choose a small amount of weight, maybe even just an empty barbell, to practice your technique and get a sense of how much more weight you should add. After a few weeks of such practice, you gradually add more and more weight, until you are lifting more than you would ever dare to try before you started. The same with equanimity. Start with small, simpler issues, as you hone your skill at both meditation and equanimity.

Now, examine an event in your life. It might be current. It might be something from your past. Try to look at it objectively and not get caught in its emotional resonance. Imagine you are playing it as a YouTube video. You can pause, rewind, or fast-forward through it. It is happening there, on your screen, something you are witnessing but is not happening to you. As you examine it, think of answering these questions:

Is this an old or new issue?

What emotions is the character in the video experiencing as the event unfolds? Every emotion is relevant. While you take stock of them, remember to keep these emotions at a distance. They are happening to the character in the video. You are only here to witness the experience, to catalog what that person felt at the time.

Do these emotions affect the character later in life, or if it is a current event, in other parts of life that have nothing to do with it?

Does this issue reoccur? If so, can it be avoided? If it cannot be avoided, is there a different way the character could relate to it than the ways you are examining now? If the issue happening is necessary, are the resulting emotions just as necessary?

The purpose of these questions is to place the situation in an objective framework. To see it as it is, rather than how it might seem when filtered through deeply-felt emotions. Sometimes problems are just not as big as they seem at first. It's like watching a scary movie and turning off the sound. While some parts of the movie might seem scary, those drawn-out parts with frightening musical scores now seem much less frightening.

When we can see the issue objectively, we are abler to examine it and ask ourselves why we let it haunt us.

Now, you are ready to detach yourself even more from the issue. As you do so, keep in mind the warnings above. Be cautious that you do not allow your emotions to undo your work, and be careful not to let your examination of your feelings for the problem become harmful. Not remaining detached can lead to depression and feelings of despair. Be mindful and do not let this happen to you. Now, consider the following:

Bad things happen.

Good times happen as often as bad times, but neither lasts.

Existing means depending on many things outside of us which we cannot control.

No one can solve your problems for you.

The points above are blunt. They may even sound depressing. But they are important to emphasize because they help us to understand: It is pointless to feel frustrated or depressed about events we cannot control or avoid. Once we accept there are things in life we have no power over, we are less likely to be emotionally trapped by them.

Continue to be mindful and aware of the issue you are working with. Be careful your mind does not wander off into distractions. Should a distracting thought present itself, do not attempt to force it away. Acknowledge its existence, and allow it to fade away on its own by returning your attention to the focus of your meditation.

When you feel you have reached a balance and a sense of peace with the emotions you have over your issue, you can now practice equanimity. Consider the benefit of a mind at rest rather than in turmoil over your problem. Continue this as long as necessary. It will be difficult at first, but as you practice equanimity, it will become easier and easier until you are able to dismiss negative emotions over the problems in your life as they occur.

Chapter Summary. Follow these steps to come to terms with and overcome issues in your life:

Equanimity is letting go of inner turmoil caused by problems and difficulties in life.

Start with simpler, less painful issues at first.

Beware of becoming distracted.

Accept the inevitability of life.

Continue until you have come to terms with your issue and when you no longer carry its emotional burden.

Chapter 13: How To Think About Failure And Risk The Healthy Way

Earlier, we discussed the powerful impact that just being a little more logical about stress at work could have. We then looked at the law of attraction and at how this makes you far more successful over time as people look at you as the person who is calm and in control.

But why is this? Why is it that most people aren't better able to control their emotions and stay calm? Why is 'panic' our default response?

The answer is that our emotions have evolved in a much more dangerous time than we live in today. We are naturally risk averse because that is the attitude that would have given us the best chance of survival out in the African Savanah.

Let's say you see an animal on the horizon and you don't know if it's a cat or a lion. In the wild, it really wouldn't make sense to treat the unknown as a cat. Rather, it makes much more sense to assume the worst and to run.

But today that's just not the case. Today, the 'worst case scenario' is really not that bad and is certainly not severe enough to put you in physical risk. The worst case scenario is your boss shouting at you, or a short period of financial hardship.

Risk aversion then is what gives you your advantage once you can get over it and it's what will help you to seem the calmest and to make the 'brave' decisions. At the same time, it can be very beneficial to apply a little cognitive restructuring in order to change the way you perceive risks and challenges more generally. Think of these as opportunities to learn and to grow, to become stronger, and to give life some interest and excitement. When you look at them like this, you'll be able to thrive rather than collapse under pressure. Very often, it's taking risks to ask someone out, invest in money, quit your job and start your own business, propose to your partner… all these things that give life meaning and color. And even if they go wrong, at least you tried.

And if you don't learn to perceive challenges this way? Then the stress will never go away. There's always an underlying sense of stress because that's human nature. The hedonic treadmill is a state of perpetual discomfort that we all tend to fall back to, even when times are good. It's what is believed to keep us working and trying but an unfortunate side effect is that we are never quite content and never able to really try anything bold and brave.

The REAL risk is that we stay frozen by fear, or that we stayed weighed down by all the admin of everyday life. The real danger is that you stay doing the same job that you don't enjoy every single day and that you never experience the contentment, the challenge or the beauty that life has to offer. That's what you should be stressed about and you should use that to push you towards your goals – even when life is hard and life is stressful. As the old expression goes: it's easier to ask for forgiveness than permission. There's never a good time. So just bite the bullet and go for it!

Chapter 14: Leave Them Behind

Have you ever heard the following phrase before? "You are the average of the 5 people and books you spend your most time with". I totally believe in this statement. If you hang around with negative people who are complaining all the time, chances are you'll also start complaining. If you spend all days of the week filling your head with negative information about death, destruction, a war is coming, etc. You're not going to feel so good. So this chapter is about leaving the people and things behind that don't support you anymore. It's not to say that you are better than them. (Even if I kind of want to think you are if they are really negative people, anyways.) To keep you grounded to have the following story instead of that, you're some much better than them: "You are simply on a different journey than they are right now".

If you are serious about overcoming anxiety, then there could be some people in your life that are preventing you from doing this. So the first thing to do is to really take the time to reflect. Are there any people in your life that make you feel bad? Maybe they are using subtle noises or gestures when you have accomplished something that you're proud of. Really take the time to feel and be honest with yourself. Whom could you get rid of? What habit could you get rid of? How do you feel after reading the newspaper? You might be addicted to it, but is it a good addiction? If you are getting negative emotions from watching or reading the news then my suggestion to you, is to stop. Personally, I read or watch the news maybe once a year, unless it gets thrown at me from someone else. Don't worry about not being updated on what's happening in the world. Instead, choose to focus on what's happening in YOUR world. Always know that you are responsible for your input. If you read positive and uplifting books, then chances are you'll become a positive person.

I truly hope that you'd take this part serious and begin to eliminate the negative forces in your life. You are a warrior of peace now, remember that. You should rather want to be alone than around negative people who leaves you with a bad feeling. Even if they are good to you from time to time, is it really worth it? I understand that it might be painful, but cut them loose. I understand that this might be hard if it's a family member. But you can always choose to spend less time with them.

So what are some action steps that you can take to begin to shift your surroundings? Well the first step is to become aware, which I believe you are now. The second step is to become ruthless. When a person discourages you, leave them. You don't need them anymore. You are better than that. You value yourself high enough to walk away from these people. Begin to show people that you don't accept their behavior towards you anymore. Chances are if they love you, then they'll change their behavior towards you. Otherwise don't feel bad about leaving them, your life is too precious. Step number three is to identify the bad habits in your life. For example, you might have a habit of reading in forums which really aren't supportive. Or maybe you watch a certain reality show that makes you feel bad. Begin to identify how you feel when you are doing your daily activities. This does not apply to everything but I think you get the point. If you are anxious when doing the dishes for example, then it's not the activity that is bringing you the feeling, it's something within you. In such a situation just remember what we've talked about in this book.

Key takeaways:

- Remember that you are the average of the 5 people you spend most of your time with.
- Leave people that discourage you. You don't need them anymore. You should rather want to be alone, than around people who makes you feel bad.
- Identify bad habits in your life and begin to eliminate them. What activities make you feel bad? Maybe it's reading the newspaper or watching a certain reality show. Stop caring so much about what's happening in the world and begin to care more about what's happening in YOUR world.

Chapter 15: 7 Mindfulness Techniques To Remain Mindful At Any Given Moment

These techniques are entirely different from the previous chapter. While the former ones offered us an opportunity to experience instant mindfulness, these techniques need time, patience and consistent practice. But the benefits they offer are simply substantial and enchanting! All we have to do is to set aside a couple of minutes for the practice, stick to the technique we choose and practice religiously every day, irrespective of the scenario!

And, within days, we will be able to feel the enormous shift in our energy levels. We will notice that we are so mindful that we have oodles of time left with us... We have that **'extra hour'** for everything... Our productivity has improved... our health is in the best-ever state!

Here are 7 such lovely techniques we can practice to instill mindfulness and enjoy stress-free lives!

1. Yin Yoga

Yoga, these days, has become synonymous with an exercise regimen where one focuses more on the physical benefits it renders. But, alas, it has much more to offer us! Yin Yoga, propagated by Paul Grilley and Sarah Power, is a gentle, yet energizing form of yoga practice that helps us to connect with our breathing. The postures are typically held for 5 to 7 minutes, without exerting stress on our bodies. The practice uses lots of props, including bolsters, blocks, blankets and straps. There are about 45 poses in a typical Yin Yoga class lasting for 90 minutes.

Here is one pose I do daily to help me remain mindful throughout the day – **The Sphinx and Seal!**

Benefits

Awakens the back, digestive system and all the organs and muscles

Gives your spine a good massage, relaxing the spine, energizing and preparing us for the whole day

Prop: Bolster

There are two poses. The first one is the Seal, in which we are lying on the belly, legs extended backward, arms placed in front of us folded into a pillow for resting our foreheads. The next one is the Sphinx. A subtly more active pose, it is a whole body stretch.

Let's see how to do both.

Lie down on the stomach, clasping the elbows with opposite hands. Adjust the hands so that elbows are resting slightly away from the shoulders. Spread the legs out slightly wider than the hips. Do not collapse completely, but make sure that the abdomen is resting completely on the mat/floor. Gaze down and hold the posture, the Seal, for about 5 minutes. Focus on your breathing. With each conscious inhalation, move the chest forward. With each exhalation, let the chest fall down. Notice how this feels on your lower back.

Now, gently slide the palms away from the body, stretching the arms completely. Make sure that the elbows are straight. Press the palms firmly into the mat/floor, and gently push the chest away from the floor, giving the abdomen a good stretch. Hold the posture, the Sphinx, for 5 minutes. Breathe in the same way as we did with the Sphinx.

Just observe the thoughts that arise in your mind as the postures are held. Do not judge. Do not criticize. But if the mind wanders away, restore the focus by bringing the attention back to your breathing.

To come out, slowly lower the chest to the floor. Turn the head to one side and rest the cheek on the palms.

We can use a bolster to support the arms if we feel that the back is hurting.

Caution: Refrain from practicing this posture if you have a lower back injury or if you are pregnant.

2. Corpse Pose And Yoga Nidra

Yes, corpse pose or Savasana is the ultimate pose for relaxation and unwinding, but it is also one of the best poses to learn mindfulness. Yoga Nidra is often practiced by lying down in this posture, which is quite often practiced as guided meditation to help us release muscle tension, lower blood pressure, slow down the heart rate and regulate breathing. We are blissfully asleep, yet we will be fully conscious without any judgment or criticism.

Lie down with the back resting on the floor. Stretch the hands away from the body, giving enough space for armpits to breathe. Separate the legs wider than the hips and allow the feet to fall to the sides. Close the eyes.

Allow the body to relax completely.

Become aware of the natural spontaneous breath that moves in and out of the body effortlessly. Feel the breath flowing in and out through both nostrils.

Slow down the breathing; lengthen and deepen the inhalations and exhalations.

Long slow inhalations followed by longer slower exhalations. Pause for a moment when the body suspends the breath.

Repeat for 15 rounds and then restore the natural, spontaneous breathing. Notice the difference.

Now, state to yourself your intention behind practicing this Yoga Nidra. In this case, it will be mindfulness/conscious awareness. Repeat it clearly and with complete awareness thrice.

Now, slowly and clearly begin a mindful journey of sensory awareness, moving gently through each and every part of the body. Begin the journey with the right side. Here is a sample which you can follow.

"Right hand thumb ... 2nd finger ... 3rd finger ... 4th finger ... 5th finger ... palm of the hand ... back of the hand ... wrist ... forearm ... elbow ... upper arm ... shoulder ... armpit ... waist ... hip ... thigh ... knee ... calf ... ankle ... heel ... sole of the foot ... top of the foot ... right big toe ... 2nd toe ... 3rd toe ... 4th toe ... 5th toe.

Left hand thumb ... 2nd finger ... 3rd finger ... 4th finger ... 5th finger ... palm of the hand ... back of the hand ... wrist ... forearm ... elbow ... upper arm ... shoulder ... armpit ... waist ... hip ... thigh ... knee ... calf ... ankle ... heel ... sole of the foot ... top of the foot ... left big toe ... 2nd toe ... 3rd toe ... 4th toe ... 5th toe.

Now go to the back of the body ... right heel ... left heel ... right calf ... left calf ... right thigh ... left thigh ... right buttock ... left buttock ... lower back ... middle back ... upper back ... the entire spine ... right shoulder blade ... left shoulder blade ... back of the neck ... back of the head.

Top of the head ... forehead ... right temple ... left temple ... right ear ... left ear ... right eyebrow ... left eyebrow ... middle of the eyebrows ... right eye ... left eye ... right nostril ... left nostril ... right cheek ... left cheek ... upper lip ... lower lip ... both lips together ... chin ... jaw ... throat ... right collarbone ... left collarbone ... right side of the chest ... left side of the chest ... upper abdomen ... navel ... lower abdomen ... right groin ... left groin ... the pelvic floor.

The whole right leg ... whole left leg ... whole right arm ... whole left arm ... the whole face ... the whole head ... the whole torso ... the whole body ... the whole body ... the whole body."

Now imagine opposite sensations. Here, we will be practicing only stress/calm.

Imagine and experience events that once caused anxiety, intense anxiety and worry. Feel this stress in the body, breath and mind, but do not focus on the source or do not try to judge the feelings or try to shoo them away. Let them come and go away naturally. Just observe. Visualize and experience the stress as vividly as possible. Now allow the feeling of calm to surround us. Visualize and experience the calmness and serenity in your entire mind, body, breath and emotions. We are relaxed and aware, we are completely calm.

Once ready, repeat the intention again.

For about one minute, allow your attention to be aware of the smooth, slow, serene flow of the breath. Let the mind make a gentle, conscious effort to guide your breathing so that it is smooth, calm, deep and without any noise or jerkiness.

To come out, gently move the toes and fingers. Roll the neck gently from side to side. Bring the focus back to normal breathing. Take 9 rounds of deep inhalations and exhalations. Stretch the arms over the head and interlock the fingers so that palms face away from you. Point the toes and give the body a good, deep stretch. Keep the eyes closed.

Turn to the right and lie down for a couple of seconds. When ready, sit up in any comfortable posture.

Rub the palms to generate heat. Place the palms on the eyes to spread the warmth. Gently open the eyes and look into the palms.

How are you feeling?

3. Trataka Meditation

It is a single pointed gazing meditation which is quite often said to improve concentration and focus. It is a great way to learn mindfulness and calm your stressed body and mind. Its secret lies in the power of constantly gazing at an object of your attention, without allowing the mind to wander. Bring the mind back to the focal point, if it wanders away.

Sit erect, keeping the body relaxed.

Place a burning candle one or two feet away from the eyes at the same level of the eyes.

Take 10 rounds of deep inhalations and exhalations to relax the body and mind and prepare it for the practice.

Once you are ready, gaze at the bright spot of the flame just above the wick. Never gaze at the top of the flame as it could flicker, disturbing your concentration.

Gaze at the flame without blinking the eyes.

Let the thoughts arise and fall away… let the mind continue its hopping from one thought to the next, but do not go behind those thoughts. Do not try to analyze the reason or aftermath. We may feel that we are being pulled away by the flow of thoughts, but just try to bring the focus back to the flame.

With practice, one can go from few seconds to few minutes without blinking. As we practice, we will see that we will be aware of only the flame. We will lose body consciousness and will feel that we are one with the flame.

Once the eyes become tired, close them gently and wait until they are completely relaxed. Meanwhile, try to visualize the flame in the space in between the eyebrows. Keep the eyes closed as long as this flame burns.

Once ready, gently open the eyes. Feel free to blink a few times to relieve any strain.

4. Thankfulness Meditation

Being grateful is one of the best things in this world. When we are mindfully thankful for each and everything in this world, we become compassionate. We become more aware of whatever is happening within us and around us. We will stop judging and criticizing, leaving zero scope for stress to step into us.

There are many ways of doing this. One of the simplest ways is to journal before you hit your bed.

Sit down in a comfortable place and posture of your choice where you will not be disturbed for the next 15 to 20 minutes. Keep your book and pen ready.

Turn off your computer and phone. Turn off your television. Make sure that you are free from any and all kinds of distractions.

Close your eyes and take 10 deep breaths to prepare your body, mind and soul for this activity.

Once you are ready, open your eyes, and slowly start writing... You can start thanking the God/Higher Self for giving you another day to live.

Do not try to criticize the moments/experiences you had on a particular day. Instead, be thankful for all those moments. Do not scorn... do not get angry... do not become upset.

Just try to be grateful for each and every second... each and every thing you went through in any given day!

If you find that your mind is loitering away and running behind a particular scenario, coax it to come back and complete the activity.

It need not be a huge list, but make sure that you are doing it with complete awareness that is free from all kinds of judgments and criticisms.

Once you complete, close the book and put it aside.

Close your eyes once again and feel the gratitude flowing out of you from your heart and filling you up with a sense of relaxation. Feel the stress flowing away and calmness filling up!

You may find it difficult to thank every moment as criticisms are pretty common, but do not lose hope! Keep practicing!

5. Loving Kindness Meditation

It is also known as compassion meditation. Most of us are so prone to harsh self-criticism that we often forget that we have to love and be kind to ourselves, thus slipping into the autopilot mode. This simple meditation will help to revive the feelings of self-love and compassion for ourselves which would help us to become more mindful.

Sit or lie down in a comfortable position.

Close your eyes and take 10 to 15 slow, long breaths to relax your body and mind and prepare it for the journey.

Allow the body and mind to center and ground so that it dwells on the present. You can place your right palm in the center of your chest to bring your awareness back as well as to remind yourself that you have love and compassion for yourself.

Feel your breath move through your body, and if your attention wanders, bring the focus back to the gentle movement of your breath once again.

After a few minutes you will start noticing any physical sensations of stress that you may be holding in your body, perhaps in your neck, jaw, belly or forehead.

Notice the difficult emotions such as worries about your future or pain from the past. Just let them go away. Release them without any attachments, judgments and criticisms.

Slowly, bring your attention towards yourself. Visualize yourself offering words of kindness and compassion to yourself, slowly and affectionately.

You can use the following affirmations:

I am safe.

I am peaceful.

I am kind to myself.

I love and accept myself as I am.

If you notice that your mind is wandering, bring it back gently to the sensations you are experiencing in your body and to the loving-kindness phrases.

If you feel entrapped in the whirlpool of emotions, free yourself from it by bringing your focus back to your breathing. Once you are comfortable again, repeat the phrases.

Once you feel you are ready, take 9 deep breaths and allow your body, mind and soul to rest, relax and rejuvenate.

Gently open your eyes.

You may find it a little confusing initially, but try to stick to the practice!

6. Forgiveness Meditation

This meditation is pretty similar to the Thankfulness Meditation. The sole difference is that instead of giving gratitude, you will be using the words "I am willing to forgive". Forgive all the incidents, persons and moments that have caused you pain or uneasiness, in the present and past.

Sit down in a comfortable place and posture of your choice where you will not be disturbed for the next 15 to 20 minutes. Keep your book and pen ready.

Turn off your computer and phone. Turn off your television. Make sure that you are free from any and all kinds of distractions.

Close your eyes and take 10 deep breaths to prepare your body, mind and soul for this activity.

Once you are ready, open your eyes and slowly start writing… Start by forgiving yourself.

Do not try to criticize the moments/experiences you had. Instead, choose to forgive yourself for any and all those moments/activities which you still experience unforgiveness for. Do not scorn... do not get angry... do not become upset.

Just try to go through each and every person... each and every thing you went through in any given day!

When your mind wanders away, bring the focus back to the breathing.

It need not be a huge list, but make sure that you are doing it with complete awareness that is free from all kinds of judgments and criticisms.

Once you complete, close the book and put it aside.

Close your eyes once again and feel the stress flowing away and calmness filling up!

"You cannot forgive just once, forgiveness is a daily practice," as the saying of Sonia Rumzi goes. **So do it daily!**

7. Mirror Body Scan Meditation

Mirror is a powerful tool that will help you to adopt mindfulness in your life. You don't have much to do here. Just stand or sit in front of a mirror and just observe your body… Just notice the way your emotions, thoughts and body react as you scan your entire body!

Sit or stand in the most comfortable way in front of a full-sized mirror.

Take 5 to 9 deep, long and slow breaths to relax your body and mind.

Take a long, deep inhalation and scan your entire body.

Do not be wary about the non-stop thoughts your mind is churning. Do not become frantic. Just keep breathing and repeat this ten times.

Notice the way your body, mind and soul respond as you completely scan your body, from head to toe. Your mental commentary is bound to trigger a fleet of negative responses and emotions in you. And, if that happens, bring the focus back to the breathing and say, "I accept myself completely as I am."

Just note the reactions without responding... You may want to note down the reaction. Please feel free to do so... It will help you understand the way your mind is churning all the unnecessary stuff...

Repeat for about 5 to 7 minutes, thrice or four times a day!

You are bound to be encompassed by a fleet of thoughts like "Oh, I wish that tummy was a little more toned" or "If my skin was glowing" etc... But do not be frightened... Just keep repeating that you accept yourself completely... Do not judge... Do not criticize. Just be "as is" and in time, you will be able to accept yourself and learn to be mindful!

Now that we have seen different ways of learning mindfulness, let's take a deeper look at what Mindfulness Meditation is all about!

Chapter 16: Eliminating Stress

When we are stressed out, we limit our capacity to act natural. Stress puts our mind in a state of perpetual worry and we become a pain to be around. Mindfulness plays a critical role in stress reduction through the following ways.

Taking our alone time

Sometimes in order to eliminate stress, we have got to pull away. When we seclude ourselves, we get re-energized. Our stress might have stemmed from taking on too much work which causes tremendous noise in our brains. Taking time alone also helps us critique our past actions. We become aware of the cause and effect. There's certainly a chain of actions behind every episode of stress that we battle against. Taking time alone allows us to investigate our actions and unravel the patterns behind our present circumstances and additionally take care not to repeat the same.

Becoming aware of the true nature of our thoughts

When we are consumed by the hassle of day-to-day living, it can be quite difficult to get in touch with our thoughts. Not a single thought lasts enough for us to decode it. But through practicing mindfulness, we come to appreciate the true nature of our thoughts. If we have been feeling uncomfortable for the most part of the day, we may be at the verge of a major depressive disorder, but it won't be obvious until we pay our thoughts close attention.

No immediate reactions

Kneejerk reactions worsen — instead of helping the situation. But if we develop the habit of taking our time before giving a response to anything, we put ourselves in an advantageous position. But it takes tremendous practice to be able to witness something and then delay your response. Mindfulness teaches us the value of taking our time to respond. This makes it certain that we are sure of what we are doing and understand the possible results. If we take actions without thinking of the results, we make ourselves vulnerable and are at risk of becoming more stressed than before.

Puts us more in touch with our body sensations

Our body is a complex living organism. It communicates in numerous ways. For instance, when your body experiences challenges in a certain area, it may send out a pain. At the onset of a problem, the pain is going to be small, but as the problem grows big, it will become worse. When we are lost in the sea of activities characteristic of our lives, it can be quite difficult to be alive to this pain right away. Mindfulness allows us to be in touch with our body and thus we are likely to detect the sensations early enough and take remedial actions.

Noticing the energy vampires

What many people haven't woken up to yet is the fact that the people we hang out with could be the indirect cause of our distress. Have you ever noticed that there are some people as soon as you meet them your emotions turn from good to worse? As long as they are in close physical proximity, they leave you feeling drained of energy and stressed out. Such people are known as energy vampires. You should cut off ties with them, and if it's impossible, try to distance yourself. But you first need to develop your capacity of detecting energy vampires. You can develop this ability by engaging in various mindfulness exercises. And once you acquire this skill, you will not only be in a position to fight off the stress induced by energy vampires, but you will also develop the capability to detect people's emotions on the whole.

Reaching out

You would have to be a god to handle your life problems on your own. The simple fact is that you need people. You can never pull through on your own and if you somehow managed to, the fulfillment wouldn't be as great as if you had people along with you. Sometimes you can be stressed out because of a lack of meaningful relationships. In such a case, the only answer is to seek people and make connections. Then you can be stressed out because your plans – one by one – have been tumbling down into a messy pile. When you reach out to people, you will not only cope with your stress but also get a solution to your problems that will ultimately get rid of your stress. Mindfulness teaches us how to connect with other people and utilize our capabilities for mutual benefit.

Gratefulness

We may not readily admit to it, but greed is almost embedded in the human DNA. We live for the next high, the next kill, the next fat check, and we never tire of it. When we are unable to secure our selfish wants, we can easily fall into depression. This attitude of always wanting more sets us up for a major disappointment once we fall short of our expectations. But when we take a moment to be grateful, we cancel out our negative thoughts, worries, and stress. Gratefulness doesn't happen out of the blue. It is a mindset that must be tended to. Mindfulness puts us into the right headspace of practicing gratefulness.

Getting physical

Scientific studies back up the fact that engaging in physical activity will cause our brain to release chemicals that banish stress. There are various ways of engaging in physical activities. We may opt to go to the gym, work out from the comfort of our homes, or engage in energy-intensive labor. When you sweat it out, you can be sure that the stress is going to subside. And mindfulness promotes the habit of working out.

Chapter 17: Eliminating Stress

When we are stressed out, we limit our capacity to act natural. Stress puts our mind in a state of perpetual worry and we become a pain to be around. Mindfulness plays a critical role in stress reduction through the following ways.

Taking our alone time

Sometimes in order to eliminate stress, we have got to pull away. When we seclude ourselves, we get re-energized. Our stress might have stemmed from taking on too much work which causes tremendous noise in our brains. Taking time alone also helps us critique our past actions. We become aware of the cause and effect. There's certainly a chain of actions behind every episode of stress that we battle against. Taking time alone allows us to investigate our actions and unravel the patterns behind our present circumstances and additionally take care not to repeat the same.

Becoming aware of the true nature of our thoughts

When we are consumed by the hassle of day-to-day living, it can be quite difficult to get in touch with our thoughts. Not a single thought lasts enough for us to decode it. But through practicing mindfulness, we come to appreciate the true nature of our thoughts. If we have been feeling uncomfortable for the most part of the day, we may be at the verge of a major depressive disorder, but it won't be obvious until we pay our thoughts close attention.

No immediate reactions

Kneejerk reactions worsen — instead of helping the situation. But if we develop the habit of taking our time before giving a response to anything, we put ourselves in an advantageous position. But it takes tremendous practice to be able to witness something and then delay your response.

Mindfulness teaches us the value of taking our time to respond. This makes it certain that we are sure of what we are doing and understand the possible results. If we take actions without thinking of the results, we make ourselves vulnerable and are at risk of becoming more stressed than before.

Puts us more in touch with our body sensations

Our body is a complex living organism. It communicates in numerous ways. For instance, when your body experiences challenges in a certain area, it may send out a pain. At the onset of a problem, the pain is going to be small, but as the problem grows big, it will become worse. When we are lost in the sea of activities characteristic of our lives, it can be quite difficult to be alive to this pain right away. Mindfulness allows us to be in touch with our body and thus we are likely to detect the sensations early enough and take remedial actions.

Noticing the energy vampires

What many people haven't woken up to yet is the fact that the people we hang out with could be the indirect cause of our distress. Have you ever noticed that there are some people as soon as you meet them your emotions turn from good to worse? As long as they are in close physical proximity, they leave you feeling drained of energy and stressed out. Such people are known as energy vampires. You should cut off ties with them, and if it's impossible, try to distance yourself. But you first need to develop your capacity of detecting energy vampires. You can develop this ability by engaging in various mindfulness exercises. And once you acquire this skill, you will not only be in a position to fight off the stress induced by energy vampires, but you will also develop the capability to detect people's emotions on the whole.

Reaching out

You would have to be a god to handle your life problems on your own. The simple fact is that you need people. You can never pull through on your own and if you somehow managed to, the fulfillment wouldn't be as great as if you had people along with you. Sometimes you can be stressed out because of a lack of meaningful relationships. In such a case, the only answer is to seek people and make connections. Then you can be stressed out because your plans – one by one – have been tumbling down into a messy pile. When you reach out to people, you will not only cope with your stress but also get a solution to your problems that will ultimately get rid of your stress. Mindfulness teaches us how to connect with other people and utilize our capabilities for mutual benefit.

Gratefulness

We may not readily admit to it, but greed is almost embedded in the human DNA. We live for the next high, the next kill, the next fat check, and we never tire of it. When we are unable to secure our selfish wants, we can easily fall into depression. This attitude of always wanting more sets us up for a major disappointment once we fall short of our expectations. But when we take a moment to be grateful, we cancel out our negative thoughts, worries, and stress. Gratefulness doesn't happen out of the blue. It is a mindset that must be tended to. Mindfulness puts us into the right headspace of practicing gratefulness.

Getting physical

Scientific studies back up the fact that engaging in physical activity will cause our brain to release chemicals that banish stress. There are various ways of engaging in physical activities. We may opt to go to the gym, work out from the comfort of our homes, or engage in energy-intensive labor. When you sweat it out, you can be sure that the stress is going to subside. And mindfulness promotes the habit of working out.

Chapter 18: Powerful Habit Changes For A Better Life

You are now fully aware of just how much our brains rely on habits to get us through our daily lives. You have also come to understand how you can use such habits to help you have a better quality of life by creating habits that are going to help you become more mindful in your everyday existence. Now, it is time for you to understand how you can create, shift, and adapt your existing habits to become even more mindful.

Leveraging your habits as a way to improve mindfulness is a powerful opportunity for you to work closely with your brain's natural tendencies so that you can experience even more mindfulness in your everyday life. When it comes to making changes in your life, especially when it comes to the way that you live your life or the lifestyle that you lead, it is important to know how you can work together with your natural behavior to make those changes last longer. A big mistake that many people make when they are trying to make a huge lifestyle change is that they try to change the very fibers of who they are. In many cases, they even try to change the way their mind and body naturally works, which ultimately fails in the end because it is extremely difficult to go against your natural tendencies. Rather than putting so much effort in changing the way that you are, you can work together with your natural tendencies to create systems within yourself that work more effectively to help you live the life that you desire. These types of changes are easier to make, and they end up being more sustainable and longer-lasting in the long run because they are simple adaptations ofthe things that you have already been doing all along.

The chances are, you have many habits that influence the way that you live your life and the experiences that you have. We all tend to have habits around the same things in our lives, though what those habits are and how we engage with them vary from person to person. For example, we all have a habit on how we start our day, but the actual details of that habit are different, depending on who you are and the habits that you developed throughout your life. In this chapter, we are going to explore some of these common habits that we all have and how you can create habits and rituals that are going to suit your needs. As we delve into these things, I want you to remember that the emphasis will always be on adjusting **your** personal habits to suit what you are trying to achieve, rather than attempting to discard your habits entirely and start fresh. Again, adapting what you are already doing will always be more efficient than trying to create entirely new habits from scratch, so do not be afraid to make changes. You might need to adopt a small number of your habits at a time and gradually shift them to become desirable habits in a way that they last long. No matter what you have to do to make these changes work, trust that you are doing it in the right way for yourself. You just have to listen to your body and your personal needs as you go.

Your Morning Habits

All of us have habits that we engage in each morning, right from the minute we wake up and until we officially start our first task of the day, such as leaving for work or class. Your morning habits can have a huge impact on your everyday life, as you already know, so having a strong set of habits that you engage in each morning can help you have a better day by improving your mood and helping you achieve more throughout the day.

Your morning routine is a great opportunity for you to create mindful habits that are going to help you set the rest of your day in positivity. When it comes to creating a mindful morning routine for yourself, it is helpful to consider what needs to be accomplished in order for you to get the most out of your routine. Each person is going to need something different based on what they do every day. For example, if you have a career that starts early in the day and requires high physical exertion, you are going to need to wake up early and have a nourishing routine that helps prepare you for a day of physical work. Alternatively, if you have a career that requires you to work from home, you are going to need to have a morning routine that motivates you to get started so that you can get the job done. Knowing what you need from your morning routine is going to help you ensure that all the elements of your routine are geared toward helping you get started with your day in the best way possible.

Once you know what you need from your morning routine, it is ideal to create an outline of what you would like to accomplish. Be mindful of what you need, the things that you enjoy in your morning routine, as well as the details ofyour current routine. All these pieces of information will contribute to making good choiceswhen establishinga new routine. With this in mind, consider how your current routine could be adapted to suit your needs and set you up for success for the rest of your day. Then, begin engaging in this routine on a daily basis so that you can start gaining the benefits of this routine and further adapting it to suit your needs and preferences.

Your Cooking and Eating Habits

In our society, cooking and eating have become habits that we do not really think about. In the past, it was customary for everyone to sit down to a home-cooked meal together with the family and enjoy a conversation about how each other's day went and how their day could have gone better. These days, meals are not really thought about in most households, and people do not sit down to enjoy them together like they once did. Furthermore, convenience has become customary in many homes, resulting in people eating low-quality fast foods and convenience-store foods rather than eating healthier home-cooked meals. As a result, eating has become more of a chore than a ritual that people engage in to nourish their bodies and take care of their well-being.

Transforming your own cooking and eating habits to become more mindful is a great opportunity for you to reclaim this part of your day and transform both cooking and eating into a more enjoyable activity. By addressing your cooking and eating habits properly, you can create a healthier lifestyle while also becoming more mindfully engaged in your cooking and eating routines. A great way to get started is to plan out each meal intentionally. As you cook, focus on being fully present in the experience of cooking so that you can truly engage with the activity and enjoy the peace and quiet of the experience.

When you are ready to eat, make sure that you eat mindfully. Consider the mindful meditation with the raisin, as we have discussed before, and do the same when you are eating the food that you have cooked for yourself. Eat slowly, and enjoy the appearance, smell, and texture of the food. Take your time enjoying every single bite. After you finish your meal, take some time to enjoy how it feels and the aftertaste of your meal. The more that you enjoy each part of the eating experience, the better you are going to enjoy each meal, and the more peaceful you are going to feel in your everyday life.

Your Hygienic Habits

Each of us has to maintain hygienic habits every single day in order to maintain our health. From brushing our teeth and combing our hair to showering and clipping our nails, there are many hygienic habits that we all engage in so that we can take care of our bodies and stay healthy. These habits cannot be drastically altered because they are basic habits, but they can certainly be made more enjoyable so that you have a positive time taking care of your body rather than feeling burdened to look after your well-being.

A great way to begin turning your hygienic habits into healthy, enjoyable habits is to see each experience as one that is devoted to taking care of yourself. People who genuinely enjoy in self-care enjoy activities centered around hygiene because it helps them truly dedicate some non-negotiable time to themselves and the way that they feel. During this time, they pamper their bodies and, as a result, their minds. By giving themselves a few minutes of undevoted attention for the sole purpose of taking care of themselves, one becomes mindful even when it's as simple as combing the hair. For many people, this is a refreshing opportunity to take care of themselves.

You can make your hygiene habits more mindful by slowing down and enjoying them more thoroughly. Use this as an opportunity to get to know your body and spend more time properly looking after your body and appreciating it and yourself for all that you are. Rather than rushing through a habitual process that may or may not still fit your hygienic needs, slow down and make sure that each part of the process is being done properly and is thoroughly satisfying your body's needs. You will probably find that the deeper you can immerse yourself into this self-care practice, the more relaxed you are going to feel, in addition to feeling satisfied with your self-care activities. This stems from slowing down and listening to your body, which means that it has time to work out naturally and release any stress or anxiety. Furthermore, you can take advantage of biofeedback at this point and use relaxing self-care practices that teach your body that it is safe to feel comfortable and relaxed, which will naturally help ease up any stress or anxiety that you may be experiencing.

Your Work Habits

We all have habits revolving around our working experiences that contribute to how we show up to work, how we partake in our daily activities, and how we complete the stuff that we are expected to complete on a day-to-day basis. When it comes to your work habits, knowing what your habits are and how they are serving your success is important. For many people, unless their habits have been addressed and they choose to create healthier habits for their work-lifemindfully, they find themselves actually creating and engaging in habits that are likely to hold them back from achieving any significant level of success in their career. This is because the mind craves efficiency and slacking certainly seems to be the most efficient way to make it through the day without exerting too much energy or expecting too much from ourselves.

When it comes to your own work habits, it can be hard to admit to yourself whether or not you are slacking at work, especially if you think that you should take pride in the work that you do. That being said, it is important that you are honest with yourself when your behavior is holding you back from achieving greater success in your career. This way, you can begin to create new habits that are going to help you excel and achieve your work goals while also feeling less stressed over your journey to success.

After you have honestly addressed what needs to be done for you to have greater success in your career, you need to begin identifying habits that are going to help you become more successful. These habits could be anything from showing up to work early to starting your daily tasks right away. Good habits can also include putting a greater effort into every report that you write,completing meticulously every project assigned to you, and submitting the highest quality of work to your superior. As you create these new habits, be mindful of how you are affected by the habits and how they benefit you. Having this mindfulness will help you create new habits that are going to serve you for years to come while also helping you remain engaged in the present moment as you carry out these mindful habits.

Your Hobby and Fun Habits

In our society, a common habit that people have developed is engaging in their hobbies as a way to bypass the stress that they experience in their lives. People binge-watch TV for hours on end, play video games for far too many hours, and obsess over their hobbies and certain forms of entertainment as an opportunity to cope with the stress that comes from work or elsewhere in their lives. While hobbies and fun activities can certainly help lower stress levels, they should not be used to avoid stress. At best, they should be used as a temporary distraction to help you relax before going back to doing the tasks that cause stress to identify a long-term solution and move forward in a more intentional manner.

When it comes to creating habits around your hobbies and the activities that you find to be fun, the first habit that you need to address is the reason for engaging in these hobbies. If you pursue these hobbies and activities to create genuine fun and maintain a healthier state of mind, then there is nothing that you truly need to address or change in your activities. If you are engaging in your hobbies and fun experiences because you are trying to avoid dealing with other more challenging parts of your life, however, you need to address the trigger that is causing you to engage in those hobbies. In this case, you need to create a new trigger that encourages you to engage in your hobbies, as well as a new habit that allows you to cope with stress elsewhere in your life. This way, when you pursue your hobbies and enjoy fun activities, you are doing so mindfully and in a way that allows you to immerse in the experience. This is in contrast to pursuing these activities because you are running away from something else.

Another way to improve your habits around your hobbies is to ensure that you are scheduling a time for these experiences on a regular basis. If you do not, you tend to find a way to squeeze them in your schedule, even if you do not actually have enough time for them. This results in feeling even more stressed out. Having adequate time to engage in your hobbies and to have fun means that you can fully become present at the moment and enjoy those fun experiences.

Allowing yourself to immerse into your hobbies fully means that you can truly let go of everything else going on in your life and fully engage in the process of fun without feeling like you are avoiding anything in your life. This way, you can be mindful of each step in the process and deeply enjoy the entire experience.

Your Alone Time Habits

The last habit that you really need to address when it comes to creating healthier habits that support your mindfulness would be your alone timehabits. Alone time is a vital experience that we all need to have in our lives to give ourselves the opportunity to experience relief from the external world. This is our time to relax, step away from our environment, and simply enjoy spending time alone with ourselves. Although some people claim not to enjoy this, psychologists argue that alone time is crucial in helping us live our lives as fully independent and happy human beings. People who know how to be alone and enjoy that time tend to be happier because they do not rely on other people, things, or circumstances to feel happy.

Creating habits around spending more time alone, doing what you love, and genuinely relaxing away from the rest of the world are all important. Even if you are only spending an hour or two each week doing something that you love, you are nurturing this part of yourself that needs to experience this independence and space away from others. This way, you are able to recalibrate and feel more appreciative and thankful for the people around you. Furthermore, your body and brain have the opportunity to relax fully and release the feelings of overstimulation that can come from spending too much time around other people and stressful activities. As a result, you will feel a lot less edgy and stressed out around other people in your life when you get to recharge, and you will have an easier time mindfully enjoying the time that you spend with others, too.

When you do engage in this alone time, put effort into making the entire experience about enjoying a more mindful moment. Pay attention to how you feel, your needs, and the activities that you can pursue so that you can thoroughly fulfill your needs and feel a lot more satisfied and less stressed. You might find that, sometimes, your alone time is best spent laying on the couch relaxing, while other times, you might want to go for a walk or get a drink from your favorite café. Your time alone may also be spent reading, playing your favorite game, or just looking at the sky and enjoying a peaceful moment. Regardless of what you need, taking the time to listen to your body and fulfill your needs is going to help you make your alone time more enjoyable while also mindfully using it to destress and create a greater sense of well-being in your life.

Chapter 19: Mindfulness Meditation To Help Cope With Physical Pain

The application of mindfulness practices for patients with chronic pain and other medical conditions first began in the United States, then it started spreading across the globe. This is because an increasing number of studies continue to prove that therapies including mindfulness meditation have helped patients reduce their stress levels and cope with the pain and anxiety.

The interesting thing about mindfulness meditation is that it does not necessarily make the pain disappear. It helps the person cope with it in a positive way, instead. In other words, they start to reduce their fear of the pain and start to free their minds from it. This sense of awareness of their own pain allows them to take a step back from overwhelming negative thoughts.

For instance, they would notice that the presence of physical pain does not necessarily mean they should allow their mind to suffer as well. They will feel less lonely, scared and depressed, and more confident, forgiving and optimistic.

Now, the more a person with chronic pain meditates each day, the stronger his or her mind naturally becomes. As a result, his stress levels will lower, his immune system will improve, and he can eventually speed up the healing process.

How to Cope with Physical Pain through Mindfulness Meditation

Doctors classify physical pain into two main types - **acute** and **chronic.** Acute pain is felt once and lasts for only a short time, specifically within 12 weeks. Medicine helps provide instant relief for such pain. Chronic pain, on the other hand, is the kind that lasts for more than 12 weeks and usually causes disruptions in the person's normal, everyday life.

Whatever type of physical pain you experience at any point in your life, it is always important to take the necessary steps towards relief. That way, you can get back to the usual routines you enjoy. One of those methods that can help you cope with the pain you are currently experiencing is mindfulness meditation. What it does is it allows you to accept the pain as it happens. Maybe that sounds absurd at first, but in a while, you will understand why this can actually help you.

First, it is important to understand that pain does not equal to suffering. Pain is a natural sensation felt as part of being alive. It is something that everyone experiences every now and then. It even serves a positive purpose in your life - that is to let you know that something is wrong. Without pain, you will have a hard time finding a way to heal yourself from the underlying condition. It is like the bell being tolled in a village right before calamity ensues.

However, it is important to remember that pain does not mean you are singled out to suffer. If you believe yourself to be **suffering** from pain, then you are more likely to entertain self-defeating thoughts that will only cause further harm to your health. On the other end of the spectrum, if you deny that the pain is there, the ease of it will only last for a short while because one cannot help but **feel** the pain again.

Instead, the best way to cope with pain is to be mindful as it comes. As soon as you feel the pain, remember that it only exists in the **now.** It is part of the present moment, which makes it impermanent. By accepting this fact, you naturally become less stressed out by the pain.

The following is a short mindfulness meditation exercise that you can easily apply whenever you begin to experience pain:

Step 1: Sit or lie down in a position, which is most comfortable for you.

Step 2: Begin focusing on your breath. Even as the pain starts to ebb and flow, continue to become aware with each inhale and exhale.

Adopt a feeling of gratitude and kindness towards your nostrils, your lungs, your belly, and body for taking each breath.

Step 3: When you are ready, bring your awareness towards how the pain demands your attention. Try to associate it with mental images of a certain shape, size, color or texture.

It may be difficult at first, but as you continue to breathe, you will become less critical of it and more curious. Become an observer of the pain as it takes place, and with each sensation or emotion that comes, acknowledge it by giving a name to it.

Here is an example of what can go on in your mind as you practice mindfulness meditation to cope with the pain:

I am breathing in, and I am breathing out.

I notice the pain, I am aware that I am more than the pain.

I notice the anger rising in me, I am aware I am more than this anger.

I am aware of the sense of frustration, I am aware I am more than this frustration.

Keep in mind that while mindfulness meditation can help you cope with the pain, it is always important to seek immediate medical attention as soon as you experience it. Only after your doctor has prescribed to you the steps you need to take towards healing should you then apply meditation to cope with the pain afterwards. It is also best to consult your doctor about you considering mindfulness meditation to help you manage the pain.

Some may think that mindfulness meditation is similar to a placebo drug, or a non-reactive substance (typically called "sugar pills") given to hypochondriacs to make them feel better, or to patients in placebo-controlled drug research. However, what some researchers have noticed about those who have taken the placebo drug is that these patients will begin to feel better or even show signs of physiological improvement even after taking these pills.

The reason is that their trust and reliance on the "pills" given to them gave them the mental strength and confidence that they will be healed. This is called the "Placebo Effect" and it simply shows that your state of mind holds more power on the healing process than you think.

Of course, this certainly does not mean that mindfulness meditation should replace conventional medicine. Rather, it should be highly considered as a form of supplementary therapy that can help you cope with and possibly heal from chronic pain and other medical conditions. Naturally, it will only work if you immerse yourself wholly in the meditation for its sake, rather than to do it in the hopes that it would heal you. This is why it is important to know the true meaning of mindfulness and how to practice it without forming any expectations.

Chapter 20: Continuing Your Mindful Growth Journey

If you want to develop a mindful life and awaken to your best self, it is important to understand that you are going to be embarking on a lifelong journey, not a one-time fix up that only lasts for a short period. Just because you have come this far in addressing various areas of your life with a mindful approach, it does not mean that yourjourney is suddenly over. Instead, it simply means that you have effectively begun to lay the foundation for a strong, mindful future that is more aligned with what you desire to experience in your life. If you want to continue to find joy in all the benefits of living a mindful life, you need to educate yourself on how you can continue to live mindfully moving forward. Until now, you have been guided and directed on how and when you should be engaging with mindfulness. You have been shown the very habits that you need to address, the behaviors that you need to change, and the strategies that you need to put into place in order to live a mindful and awakened existence. Now, you need to learn about how you can identify when a situation calls for mindfulness, how mindfulness can be applied, and what you can do to live your best mindful life possible. In a sense, this is how you are going to take the leap on your own so that you can really live as freely as possible in your mindful life.

It is important that you take the time to develop these skills in your life, as not knowing how to be mindful on your own can lead you to strugglein living a mindful and awakened life. Each of our lives is so drastically different and unique that we are taken on wonderful journeys that are wildly different from the journeys that other people have. If you truly want to be more of anything in your life, you need to learn the important elements of the skill itself and not just how to apply it to specific situations. This way, when you find yourself engaging in a unique situation that you have yet to read about, you can still identify how you can apply that particular skill to that unique situation.

The steps that you are about to learn are going to take you from doing a mindful edit of your life to becoming a mindful master creator of your own life. You are truly going to awaken to your power now and find ways to begin changing your entire experience through your own personal understanding of what mindfulness is, how it works for you, and how you can personally apply it to various situations in your life.

First and Foremost, Get to Know Yourself

If you truly want to master mindfulness in your own life, you need to put effort into getting to know yourself. At the end of the day, if you do not know yourself, you are going to struggle in making mindful decisions regarding your life because you will not know which decision would serve you best. Living your life based on what other people say is only going to result in you living a life that someone else should be living and not your own life. You will end up doing everything based on what your Mom, friend, boss, or cousin would do, rather than what you would personally do. Take time to explore yourself in every way and watch how this changes your life and support you inbecoming more mindful. Spend time alone, try new hobbies, listen to different music, watch various documentaries and educational series, read books, and explore new information so that you can get to know yourself even more. This way, as you continue to grow, you will find yourself having an even deeper sense of understanding around who you are and what you can do to honor yourself in every way in your lifetime.

Conclusion

Every morning when you awaken you have a choice before you. You may allow your mind to continue sleeping with no awareness of what is happening at this very moment. You also have the opportunity to consciously awaken your inner self to the opportunities of this new day.

If you arise early enough and turn to the East you can watch the light began to break through the darkness of the night. Dawn is not a cataclysmic awakening. It begins with a hint of change pushing through. If you stay to watch you will discover that the darkness slowly dissolves and that which was hidden begins to reveal itself.

If your inner self is awake when this happens you will notice the quickening of the molecules of nature as they throw off their slumber. If you pay attention to what is happening within you, you will notice your own being vibrates to the possibilities of what this new day brings.

New choices await you. Yes, you will need to manage the aftermath from the day before, but you may now go in a new direction. The only thing preventing you is your own lack of willingness to awaken with the Dawn. You must come to realize that the routine of life many fall into is simply a retreat from accepting personal responsibility for living.

No matter how you came into this world, whether it was with love or abandonment, how you play out this life is totally up to you. To live fully with all the molecules of your being vibrating with joy, you simply need to wake up.

How do you do this? It is really rather simple. Begin with a full complete and languorous stretch. Tell your body you are ready to interface with the world in awareness. Notice everything in the room around you. Do you like it? Is it in the right place? Is there anything about it you wish to change? Look out your window or your door and asked the same questions.

What is your emotional response to what you have asked? Are you filled with excitement or dread? If with dread, what are you going to do about it? The decision is yours. There is nothing holding you back from beginning anew except your own resistance to change.

You may say, "I have responsibilities I must attend to." Yes, that certainly may be true. You may be caring or providing for people who have no one else to care for them. These may be children, spouse or partner, the elderly or infirm. How do you feel about these responsibilities? Are you able to have your internal world fulfill these obligations with joy?

When you cannot change the external circumstances surrounding you, the only thing left is to alter what you have control of. You have control over how you think and what you feel. That is a power few people understand. Do you understand how your life will change if you marshal your internal power? The details of the circumstances of your life may not change, but your internal world will open you to the possibilities that only joy can provide.

www.ingramcontent.com/pod-product-compliance
Lightning Source LLC
Chambersburg PA
CBHW072011070526
44583CB00015B/1426